ıg Women at Work

HILLC

This book is due for r

The Explorations in Feminism Collective

Jane Attala
Jane Cholmeley
Claire Duchen
Renate Duelli-Klein
Catherine Itzin
Diana Leonard
Pat Mahony
Caroline Waller

Explorations in Feminism

Close to Home
A materialist analysis of women's oppression
Christine Delphy
Edited and translated by Diana Leonard

Gender and Schooling
A study of sexual divisions in the classroom
Michelle Stanworth

Geography and Gender
An introduction to feminist geography
Women and Geography Study Group of the IBG

Going up into the Next Class
Women and elementary teacher training 1840–1914
Frances Widdowson

Helping Women at Work
The Women's Industrial Council, 1889–1914
Ellen Mappen

The Sexuality Papers
Male sexuality and the social control of women
Lal Coveney et al.

Well-Founded Fear
A community study of violence to women
Jalna Hanmer and Sheila Saunders

Helping Women at Work

The Women's Industrial Council, 1889–1914

Ellen Mappen

Hutchinson
in association with
The Explorations in Feminism Collective

London   Melbourne   Sydney   Auckland   Johannesburg

Hutchinson & Co. (Publishers) Ltd
An imprint of the Hutchinson Publishing Group

17–21 Conway Street, London W1P 6JD
and 51 Washington Street, Dover, New Hampshire 03820, USA

Hutchinson Publishing Group (Australia) Pty Ltd
16–22 Church Street, Hawthorn, Melbourne, Victoria 3122

Hutchinson Group (NZ) Ltd
32–34 View Road, PO Box 40–086, Glenfield, Auckland 10

Hutchinson Group (SA) (Pty) Ltd
PO Box 337, Bergvlei 2012, South Africa

First published 1985

Set in VIP Plantin and Perpetua by
D. P. Media Limited, Hitchin, Hertfordshire

Printed and bound in Great Britain by
Anchor Brendon Ltd,
Tiptree, Essex

British Library Cataloguing in Publication Data
Mappen, Ellen
  Helping women at work: the Women's Industrial Council
  1889-1914.—(Explanations in feminism; 8)
  1. Women's Industrial Council—History
  I. Title II. Series
  331.4'2'06041   HD6135

Library of Congress Cataloging in Publication Data
Main entry under title:

Helping women at work.

  (Explorations in feminism)
  Bibliography: p.
  1. Women in trade-unions—England—London—History. 2.
Women—Employment—England—London—History. 3.
Women's rights—England—London—History. 4. Women's
Industrial Council (Great Britain)—History. I. Mappen,
Ellen. II. Women's Industrial Council (Great Britain) III.
Explorations in Feminism Collective (Great Britain) IV. Series.
HD6079.2.G72L64 1985   331.4'09421   84-21106

ISBN 0 09 159471 5

Contents

Acknowledgements

An earlier version of the essay was presented at the Berkshire Conference on the History of Women in June 1976. I would like to thank Judith Walkowitz and Joan Burstyn for their encouragement and comments at that time. I would also like to thank Leonore Davidoff, Anna Davin, Marc Mappen, John Thane, and Pat Thane for their help and support in my efforts.

PART ONE

An Overview of the Women's Industrial Council

1 Introduction

During the closing years of the nineteenth and the early decades of the twentieth centuries, a substantial number of British women attempted to achieve a wide range of social, economic, and political rights. For the most part, historians have concentrated on suffrage efforts but in fact many of the women activists held a broader vision of feminism and placed the improvement of women's economic and social conditions alongside the struggle to obtain the vote. These women, mostly middle class in origin, banded together in societies 'looking after women'. Their efforts thus provide historical evidence for the existence of a social feminist network, part of which sought to overcome inequalities in the lives of working-class women.[1]* In so doing, they also hammered out a public role for educated women, a position long denied by the political and social system, and equally significant in the study of women's struggle for equality.

In part, the organizations which were formed in these years to further feminist concerns, took their lead from earlier efforts associated with the names of Lydia Becker, Emily Davies, Josephine Butler, Barbara Leigh Smith Bodichon and others. Although sympathetic to each other's causes, these advocates of women's rights had each organized separate campaigns to achieve political, educational, personal and property rights believed basic to the lives of women.[2] By the late 1880s, the revival of the socialist movement and the 'new unionism' provided another direction for feminist thought and action. The latter, in particular, had brought many middle-class women into contact with working-class women and girls, and thus developed a 'movement for the welfare of industrial women'.[3]

---

*Superior figures refer to the notes at the end of each chapter.

The Women's Industrial Council, founded in 1894, was a product of this radical and socialist environment in London and became a centre for social feminist commitment during the Edwardian years. Collectively, its members formed a pressure group to influence public opinion and to overcome what was later called 'masculine indifference to women's interest' through social reform methods. The main appeal of the Council was clearly stated in its Second Annual Report: it attracted 'large numbers of young women of education and intelligence' who wished to improve permanently 'the social conditions of working women'. However, this emphasis on social aspects did not limit the activities of the Council's members to one issue or group. Rather, many of its members supported the suffrage movement and also belonged to the various liberal, socialist and labourite societies which flourished in London of this period.[4]

This essay will concentrate on key aspects of the Council's twenty-five year history, focusing primarily on its period of greatest activity during the first fifteen years of its existence. Specifically, the discussion will focus on the Council's formation out of an earlier trade union organization, the Women's Trade Union Association; its emphasis on the investigation of the social and economic condition of women workers as a prerequisite to any reform efforts; and, as illustrations of the Council's agenda, a number of its activities.

What becomes apparent from a discussion of the Council's efforts between 1894 and the end of the Edwardian period is the complexity of and the inconsistencies inherent in the ideology and practice of social feminism before the First World War. By forming a pressure group, the Council's members had raised significant questions about women's function in society both for themselves and also for those they sought to help. The answers were, not surprisingly, partly shaped by nineteenth-century conceptions of both women's role and of working-class life and not purely by feminist ideals.

The Women's Trade Union Association (WTUA), formed as a result of the women's trade union movement of the late 1880s, was the immediate forerunner of the Women's Industrial Council. Interest in organizing working-class women and girls had, of course, existed long before the match girls' strike in the East End of London in 1888. The

Women's Trade Union League, founded in 1874 as the Women's Protection and Provident League, already had established between thirty and forty women's societies before Annie Besant set to work. By 1886, more than half of the League's membership was in London. The League, however, had left the task of organizing women in the East End virtually untouched.[5]

After the dockers' strike a new attempt 'to aid the working women of East London' was made. A Mrs Sheldon Amos held a meeting of a group of 'ladies' who were anxious to improve the condition of working women. As a result, a committee was formed to found and promote trade unions for women, primarily in the East End, but the possibility of organizing elsewhere was not ruled out. The committee tried to approach the League to discuss co-ordinating efforts but it appears this came to no avail. Finally, on 8 October 1889, the Women's Trade Union Association, 'to establish *self-managed* and self-supporting Trade Unions', officially came into being (my italics).[6]

The emphasis on 'self-managed' unions is worthy of further discussion. The hope of the Association, as later with the Council, was that working-class women and girls would eventually become capable of leading their own organizations. The First Report of the Association called for women of 'leisure and ability' to help in the early stages of organization. Moreover, the belief held by these social feminists that an outgroup needed the support of those who had either more practical experience, more education, more leisure, or more financial or political power can be found not just in their relationship to working-class women. For instance, they aligned themselves with men who had similar political interests and had the additional advantage of being able to vote and sit in Parliament. Even so, the women members took the initiative in forming these organizations, and as they gained more public experience, they did become the true leaders of the movement they had begun. In the same way, the theme of helping working-class women and girls to help themselves ran through many of the Association's as it would the Council's programmes. This help was not solely to be imparted by middle-class women for some members of the Association clearly had working-class ties but were accepted into a predominantly middle-class organization.

These points are illustrated by the events of the inaugural meeting and by the composition of the governing committee of the Association. First, at the meeting, John Burns, who was then on the London County Council (LCC), Tom Mann, H. H. Champion and Ben Tillet gave speeches. Burns emphasized that he was there to show the East Enders how to improve themselves and to help the women achieve what they could not do themselves. But those in attendance also heard, in a contrasting vein, from the 'intrepid Liberal', Lady Margaret Sandhurst, who said,

She had long known of the sufferings of women in the East-end, but she had been powerless to remove them. *It was the women themselves* who must remove them. They would be helped by others, and she only hoped they would be able to find a female John Burns. (Cheers). There was nothing the women of the West-end would not do to help the women of the East-end, and she hoped they would go on with the movement until they achieved what they desire.[7] (My italics.)

Further, the Radical politician Sydney Buxton became the Association's treasurer, and the governing committee included Champion, Mann, N. L. Leon, a progressive member of the LCC, W. C. Steadman, a Fabian, who was Secretary of the Barge-Builders' Union, and Stephen Fox, an investigator for Charles Booth.

In actuality, the work of and direction taken by the WTUA was in the hands of its women members, primarily under the guidance of Clementina Black. Born in 1853, the daughter of a solicitor and the Town Coroner of Brighton, Black had recently turned to trade union organizing and the work which would earn her a role as a 'leader in the women's industrial movement'. Her first efforts to be a 'public' figure were as a writer of romantic fiction, but she also became an active Fabian and Secretary of the Women's Trade Union League. The last occurred in 1886 after the death of its founder, Mrs Emma Paterson. Black worked with the League until May 1889 when she resigned and then joined the attempt to organize women in the East End through the WTUA.[8]

Black's involvement with the League and then, after 1889, with the Women's Trade Union Association opened her eyes to the problems of women workers. As she wrote in 1889, she was shocked and horrified at what she saw in the East End. Black previously had no knowledge of the low wages paid to girls and women. She declared at that time that low pay was 'at the root of most of the wrongs and sufferings of working women in this country'.[9] At a later date, she would stake her leadership position in the Women's Industrial Council by supporting trade boards to regulate wages.

Black was aided in her work by women who would eventually join her on the Council. They included Mrs Amie Hicks, who became Secretary of the East London Ropeworkers' Union when it was formed by the Association. Hicks described herself as the wife of a working man, and was characterized by Ramsey MacDonald as 'a working woman of some note as a Socialist worker, with a strong motherly face, a firm independent character, a great store of good simple common sense, and, above all, the mother of children who doated upon her and admired her' (*sic*).

Hicks's eldest daughter Frances also joined her in these organizing efforts. The younger Hicks became Secretary and one of the organizers for the Association during the third year of its existence. She was subsequently nominated by the London Trades Council to sit on the Technical Education Board. Finally, she continued her alliance with Black when the Association evolved into the Council.[10]

Another woman, Clara James, became Assistant Secretary of the Association after she had been dismissed from her position in the confectionary trade for joining a union. While an organizer for the Association, she became Secretary of the Confectioners' Union and was also, for a time, the only woman delegate on the London Trades Council. Florence Balgarnie, a Liberal who became a suffragist, was on the Association's governing committee and would later join the Council.[11]

The main purpose of the WTUA was to found unions for women workers. In fulfilling this objective, the Association clearly stated that its funds were to be devoted to 'purely propagandist expenses'; that is, to such costs as hiring of halls and the printing of handbills. In addition, its funds could be used to make temporary allowances to any woman who was discharged from employment simply for joining a union, in this way offering some monetary protection to the workers being organized.

From the beginning, the committee decided that its funds definitely would not be used for strike purposes. As the annual reports and other evidence indicate, this dictum did not always prevent strikes. However, the Association's emphasis raises several points. First, the policy guaranteed that the Association's already meagre funds would not easily be depleted. More important, it underlined the middle-class nature of the Association's leadership for, at the time, the strike was viewed as a radical and working-class industrial weapon, and not as a tool for an organization led primarily by middle-class women. Rather, the Association emphasized conciliation although this was tempered by persistence in fighting for its beliefs. This approach to gain public support was later adopted by the Council.

Some of the Association's activities which foreshadowed those of its successor worth noting in illustrating its extensive involvement and, also, in part, its emphasis on instilling self-leadership in working-class girls. Frances Hicks, for example, started an evening club for union members. It was soon happily reported that the members showed 'themselves most encouragingly capable' and began to undertake more and more of the management of the club. In addition, the Association, as did the League, instructed factory hands in the provisions of the Factory and Workshop Act and joined with other women's groups to pressure the government to appoint women factory inspectors.[12]

In spite of these efforts, it is evident that by 1893 the leaders of the Association were searching for a new form of organization to improve industrial conditions for women workers. By then, they had concluded that although trade unionism was necessary, trade unions composed exclusively of women were insufficient vehicles to remedy the many grievances of working women. Whether because of harassment by employers, trade depressions, lack of interest or knowledge on the part of the public as well as the workers themselves, or because of the difficulties inherent in attempts by middle-class 'ladies' to organize working-class women and girls, the Association's efforts had not led to any permanent changes.[13] Rather, the leadership thought that a political organization which could publicize the problems faced by working women and also exert pressure on government officials to bring about change would ameliorate conditions.

A decision was made by the late autumn of 1894 to redirect the focus of the Association's activities and to ensure its permanent existence as 'an association whose aim it was to watch over the interests of women engaged in trades, and over all industrial matters which concern women'.[14] Influenced by the emphasis placed, by socialist and liberal reformers alike, on the dissemination of information about labour questions to the public, the Association called a conference on women's labour in London to establish a new organization, namely the Women's Industrial Council. During the course of the meeting, Clementina Black moved the following resolution:

That in the opinion of this conference it is desirable that a central council shall be established to organize special and systematic inquiry into the conditions of working women, to provide accurate information concerning those interests, and *to promote such action as may seem conducive to their improvement.*[15] (My italics.)

This resolution, carried by a large majority of those present, set forth the general direction followed by the Council in subsequent years. Since the Council was primarily supported and led by middle-class women, the shift from a trade union body to a fact-gathering one enabled the new organization to continue its fight for women's economic rights in a manner more socially acceptable to the middle class.

Further, as Eleanor Marx had written a few years earlier, 'Miss Black . . . has never done a day's manual labour' and thus she and other women with like backgrounds might conceivably make more of a contribution to social reform and the achievement of women's rights from the committee room than in front of a sweated workshop distributing handbills to working-class women and girls. Whether Black's social status had indeed hindered her in attempts to organize trade unions for women on a permanent basis is problematical. Black's own writings provide some insight into this question. For example, in 1907, she related how she went to visit a factory dining-room to speak to the girls who worked there. Her strangeness among them, even viewed from a distance, is apparent, and her emphasis on their 'singularly vile' language, even though she claimed to understand their situation, is somewhat telling. Whatever the case, she did lead the new organization in its research and publicity efforts so that those who cared 'anything about the social condition of women and girls' were placed 'under a great obligation' to improve these conditions.[16]

The new organization continued to attract the support of male labour and radical leaders in the metropolis. However, the fact that new women with similar social views to those already involved in the Council's activities were continually drawn to it as a vehicle for improving the life of working-class women and girls is of great note. Characteristically, most of the women were of socialist, labourite or liberal bent. For example, the Council numbered among its early members Margaret Gladstone MacDonald, who later helped found the Women's Labour League; B. L. Hutchins, the Fabian writer on women's work; Lily Montagu, the Jewish leader of girls' clubs in London; Lady Aberdeen, a leader among Liberal women; and Catherine Webb, a Liberal and leader of the Women's Co-operative Guild.

Armed with the knowledge gained by the work of its Investigation Committee, Black and the other leading Council members attempted to influence public opinion and government policy on women's issues. By 1913, the Council, still considered an ongoing and successful organization, had investigated 117 trades and had inquired into such specific topics as the conditions of home work and the work of married women. Both of these areas were matters of concern to social reformers.[17]

The Council's efforts did not end with the mere gathering of statistics, for its members actively publicized their findings and views in a variety of ways. For instance, they wrote for journals; published a small quarterly, the *Women's Industrial News (WIN)*; held numerous public conferences on women's and girls' labour, often in conjunction with other women's groups; gave lectures on subjects related to women's work; wrote legislation which was introduced by 'friends' in Parliament concerning the regulation of home work; wrote letters and organized deputations to public officials and bodies, such as the Central Committee of the London Unemployed Fund, the predecessor of the Central (Unemployed) Body for London; and appeared as witnesses before parliamentary inquiries.

As the Organizing Secretary of the London Charity Organisation Society testified in 1906 to the Poor Law Commission, the Council was one of the groups which had drawn attention 'to the conditions under which labour is carried on in the worst paid and most injurious trades' and had 'had considerable effect on influencing public opinon'. The General Secretary of the Council also noted in *Women with the Basket*, that the Council had become 'a powerful influence in progressive legislation on women's work'. Black's own reputation as the Council's 'chief inspirer' was rewarded in 1913 when she was granted a civil list pension of £75, a grant given to a 'very small number of women'.[18]

Thus, the Council's members were able to establish themselves as 'public' experts on questions related to women's work. As part of this, the Council continued to press for the employment of educated women by public authorities. Following the path begun by the Association and other women's groups, the Council continuously sought to increase the number of women factory and sanitary inspectors, school board members, medical officers and so on. The members viewed these efforts not only as another way to secure employment for women but also as a method of keeping the discussion of women's issues alive.

In some cases, Council members benefited directly. For instance, in 1905, Grace Oakeshott, a Newnham graduate and the Secretary of the Council's Technical Education Committee, was appointed as Inspector of Women's Classes on Industrial and Trade Subjects of the London County Council's Education Committee; another member, Nettie Adler, was appointed to the same Committee. A third, Helen Smith, became Lady Superintendent of the Borough Polytechnic where the first trade school was opened for girls in London, an institution for which the Council had campaigned. It does indeed seem that, in its own small way, the Council became, as its General Secretary L. Wyatt-Papworth wrote in 1914, 'a training ground for the national service'.

In changing the scope of the organization, Black, Hicks and the other women involved appear to have removed themselves from direct contact with the women and girls they sought to help. For the most part, its members were no longer practising trade unionists but social investigators, reformers and administrators, whose activities revolved around meetings, conferences, letter-writing campaigns and organizing deputations. Even so, they still saw themselves as listening to calls for help from women workers. For example, in 1902, Council members –

including Black, Webb and Lady Aberdeen, its President – engaged in 'quiet and amicable negotiations' with the Lipton Company to improve conditions of employment for women workers. They were able to obtain washing basins and an afternoon tea break, the tea to be provided free of charge by Lipton.[19]

Further, the Council was concerned about legal matters pertaining to the welfare of working women. At times, it served as an intermediary and reported violations of the Factory Acts to the inspectors. In addition, the Council acted as a 'Poor Woman's Lawyer'. It was the Council's stated function,

to assist poor women with legal aid in instituting or defending any legal proceeding which may be considered to be test cases, involving questions of principle affecting the industrial conditions or interests of women generally, or any class or section of women.

Cases referred to the Council were handled by Robert S. Garnett, a lawyer who was also a member of the Council, and ranged from industrial matters to divorce and probate-related issues.[20]

In spite of the changed emphasis, many of the Council's members still maintained direct ties with the working-class beneficiaries of its activities. This relationship was strengthened by the organization of working girls into clubs for social and educational purposes, which proved to be an important aspect of the Council's work. It was recognized as one of the principal groups in London concerned with developing the club as an institution for the welfare of girls.

Girls' clubs were one tool used by middle-class reformers to encourage leadership among working-class girls, but they had many other functions, including the improvement of the physical conditions of club members as well as the development of domestic ideals in working-class girls so that they would become better housewives and mothers. Girls' club leaders tried to provide vacations at the seaside or in the country for club participants. In 1901, Lily Montagu, who had first been introduced to club life through her friendship with Margaret Mac-Donald, along with Mary Neal and Emmeline Pethick, purchased the Green Lady Hostel in Littlehampton. The hostel, which was but ten minutes from the sea, provided a holiday home for girls of all denominations and from different clubs. Neal and Pethick had helped found the Esperance Working Girls' Club in West London in 1895.[21]

To carry on this activity and 'to obtain the confidence of the workers', the Council formed the Clubs Industrial Association in February 1899. This sector of the Council, which eventually developed into the National Organization of Girls' Clubs, aimed primarily at educating working girls in their rights and duties as citizens and in their rights as workers so that they could ultimately help themselves in their working lives. As part of these efforts, the Association organized lectures on industrial matters at affiliated girls' clubs, held bi-monthly meetings for the delegates from clubs at the Council office to discuss 'matters of industrial import', circulated copies of the Factory Acts and other literature, and set up a 'channel of communication' to report offences of the Factory Acts to the Home Office without betraying the source of information. At times, their activities had its lighter moments. For example, to provide working girls with a knowledge of the Factory Acts, Black wrote a 'Rhyme of the Factory Acts', which according to Montagu, 'aroused considerable mirth among the members of our Club'.[22]

The Clubs Industrial Association also organized 'Social Evenings', at which time talks were given and topics of interest to working girls were discussed. For example, at one such meeting in 1905, Dr Ethel Vaughn gave a talk on 'Health at Home and in the Workshop' to 127 people, including representatives from twenty-nine clubs. At another evening in 1909 at Dean Street in Soho, eighty-five girls discussed the question, 'Should the school-leaving age be raised to sixteen, and the last two years devoted to learning a trade?' The economic plight of many working-class girls was evident at this latter meeting. The *WIN* noted that 'the tone of the remarks were somewhat bitter, because the girls felt that their desire for educational advantages was rendered impracticable by their economic conditions'; this was again brought out by the topic of a later meeting which centred on dressing on £6 a year. Topics for discussion were also pertinent to the social questions of the times. At an Association meeting in December 1903, the question of physical deterioration among girls between the ages of 14 and 18 was discussed.

In the autumn of 1902, citizenship classes were established to draw girls from the various clubs into a more active participation in citizenship life by increasing their 'knowledge of questions affecting civic life' and teaching 'responsibility by encouraging them to help themselves, and each other, by understanding and obeying the industrial laws'. The activities of these classes included investigation work into trades, the study of trade unionism, the fiscal question, and the work of the borough councils, a debate on the factory laws, and the publication of a newspaper. Members of the Council, including MacDonald and Oakeshott, were involved in these efforts to educate working-class girls.

The Women's Industrial Council also developed the physical exercise side of club life through the institution of physical drill organized by Clara James. Lessons were given at any girls' club that requested them. By 1903, the *WIN* could report that the Physical Drill was so popular that it was taught in most girls' clubs. James did some of the teaching, and several of her pupils went on to become drill instructors themselves. Annual public drill displays were held to raise money and to afford the girls a chance to show off what they had learned. The displays gave the girls, according to Lady Aberdeen, a chance to wipe 'away the reproach that no woman can jump'.

These projects and proposals demonstrate the dualism inherent in the social feminist consciousness of the period, which is most apparent in another aim of the Association's leaders. The officers wanted to influence girls' future and true role in life as well as to endow them with some modicum of critical thought for their working lives. The officers did believe strongly that through education in industrial and social subjects, working girls would become more useful citizens and more efficient workers. But in the end, they would,

be better equipped for wifehood and motherhood in as much as their sense of proportion [would] be quickened through interest in the important issues of life and through the recognition of their duty to the coming generation of workers.[23]

As the result of its inquiries, Council members came to believe that most of the bad conditions of women's work had developed because of the large supply of unskilled and untrained workers. One solution was to improve technical training for girls of the working classes. Because the Council was of the opinion that existing technical education for girls was inadequate, a Technical Training Committee, headed by Oakeshott, was created in May of 1900 to study the system of technical education and to be the voice of industrial workers in demanding new programmes. The Committee issued a report in July 1902 expressing its views on possible improvements and recommending that day trade schools teaching both trade and general education subjects should be opened for girls.[24]

In 1903, the Council published a pamphlet, *Technical Education for Women and Girls at Home and Abroad*, which detailed its findings and recommendations on the subject. This publication is worthy of note because it provides some insight into the views of the Council towards the people they sought to help. Three observations are pertinent. First, the Council made a clear class distinction in the types of occupations that young girls should pursue. Its investigations had concentrated on 'those classes which were more calculated to attract girls, who on leaving elementary school would become servants or factory hands'. Technical education for middle-class girls, daughters of small shop-keepers and clerks, and even those of 'the superior artisan' consisted of training in commercial subjects – shorthand and typewriting – and teaching. But for those girls whose fathers earned – when they worked – from 20 shillings to 30 shillings per week, training in manual occupations was considered best.[25]

With this attitude, a second point followed. The Council recommended the institution of technical classes in the 'great industries peculiar to women' – that is, the domestic industries, laundry work and the needle trades. A few other small trades, such as artificial flower-making, cigar and cigarette-making, French polishing, and jewel-case lining, were also suggested. There was no attempt to institute training in men's trades. The Council accepted the traditional work structure and expressed the view that there was no sense in training women in trades in which the skilled work was already done by men. This led to the suggestion that girls be trained to become ladies' maids, nursemaids and the like. Even fifteen years later, the Council still thought that domestic service was a viable occupation for working-class women and proposed a scheme to modernize the occupation.[26]

Third, the importance of developing skills necessary for proper motherhood as well as the improved ability to find employment was highlighted as a benefit of technical education. Believing that motherhood had to be taught, the Council proposed a combination of a year's training at a domestic economy school with a year at a trade school as the ideal method of education. According to the Council, both kinds of technical training were needed by most women – one for their industrial career and the other for their home life. The Council was in the mainstream of thought in concluding that infant care should be included as part of a girl's technical education so that proper 'mothering and tending' would be given to children – the future 'citizens of the State'.[27]

To implement its beliefs, the Council finally took matters into its own hands and created an institution where girls of the industrial classes could be trained in the nursing and rearing of infants and in domestic work. It had first presented a plan to the LCC in 1898 for the training of children's nurses, but this was never adopted as a trade school subject. Still, the Council continued to discuss the need for the training of the class of girls who became nursemaids. Its members could 'imagine nothing more beneficial or helpful towards a solution of industrial questions and "woman-questions" than such a programme'.[28]

The Council finally decided to open a nursery training school at Hackney in 1911 to supplement the work of the domestic economy classes of the London County Council. It was, as MacDonald noted, 'the logical outcome' of the Council's past policy. In addition to diverting girls from already overcrowded trades, the new school, in the form of a day nursery, would, according to Black, 'make some practical contribution towards the pressing problems of Infant Mortality, by preparing at least some working-class girls for their future duties as wives and mothers'. The Council's efforts could only serve to render working-class girls 'wiser mothers and more efficient housewives'.[29]

The Women's Industrial Council had been formed to achieve economic rights for 'industrial' women and girls. Over the years, the Council's members keenly observed all matters pertaining to the lives of these women, particularly their working lives. Indeed, an article on the

Council from the *Leicester Daily Post* in 1914 was aptly titled 'Looking After Women'. In this way, the Council's history illustrates the importance of a basic feminist vision which allowed a small but active core of women to form a pressure group and to remain a factor in London politics at least until the outbreak of war in 1914.

The women who joined the Council's ranks before 1914 to help other women practised a brand of feminism that was tempered by aspects of societal, popularity called Victorian, thought about women's place in life. Although its leaders were, for the most part, independent women, many of their solutions to the problems faced by working-class women and girls were based on the premise that these women were, or would be, wives and mothers first, and workers second.

The Council's story, only some of which has been related in this essay, thus provides an opportunity to observe the working out of the conflicts in turn-of-the-century social feminism. Examples abound in the decade before the war where the Council brought the needs of a group of working-class women to the public eye only to clothe the solutions to these problems in pure Victorian rhetoric.

Yet in spite of this dualism in their vision, their version of feminism had a pragmatic bent which sets them aside from those who simply accepted the stereotypic view of women's role. Having studied the employment situation for working-class women, they realized that, at times, married women with children had to work. Black made the point in her testimony before the Select Committee on Home Work in 1907 that 'a married women works in nine cases out of ten . . . because her husband does not receive a sufficient wage to keep the family comfortable'.[30] Thus, in addition to its other functions, the Council's nursery school also provided a small day-care centre in Hackney for mothers who had to work.

The Council offered a two-pronged solution to the low wage and poor working condition problem faced by many London working-class women. First, they did insist that proper technical education for working-class girls would at least prepare a girl, and then later a woman, for entering, or re-entering, the labour market, and, they hoped, command a living wage. As early as 1894, Hicks maintained that 'unless the woman' who had to work 'is a competent worker the situation is very serious'.[31] This belief guided the Council's efforts in the area of working-class girls' education.

But this was not their only response. Rather, they looked, as did other social feminist groups at the time, to the husband, and thus called for increased wages for men so that married women would not have to seek work, at least, as Black emphasized, not while they had young children.[32] Where husbands could not find employment, the Council, in 1907, called for a more complete system to aid out-of-work men so that, again, their wives would not have to enter the labour market.[33] Indeed, the Council's scheme for unemployed women, first promulgated in 1904 and 1905, was geared only toward women who were dependent upon their own earnings. MacDonald later summed much of it up in an article she co-authored with another member of the Council, but which was published by the Women's Labour League, when she noted that a ' "Right to Work" Act for men would be a charter to the "Right to Leisure and Home Comfort" for their wives'.[34]

This concern over the male worker as well as the female worker is explained not only by the influence of Victorian ideology but also by the allegiances which Council members brought with them when they joined the Council. For the Council appears to have been a common meeting ground in London for those who were also active in or supporters of other groups, ranging from women's organizations such as the National Union of Women Workers, the Women's Labour League, the Women's Liberal Federation and the Women's Co-operative Guild to the Fabian Society, the Independent Labour Party and the Labour Party. These other interests must be considered in evaluating the Council's programmes.

The Council's emphasis on social and economic rights also did not divorce its actions from the continuing struggle to obtain the vote. For example, when the Trades Union Congress rejected a resolution on women's suffrage in 1902, the *WIN* expressed displeasure. The Council was also represented in a deputation to Campbell-Bannerman on the vote in May 1906.[35] Later, some members of the Council continued to work actively for the vote. Black held office in the National Union of Women's Suffrage Societies and in the London Society for Women's Suffrage and was an acting editor of *Common Cause*. In 1907, she was a member of a committee which collected signatures on a declaration in favour of women's suffrage, a declaration she had helped write in 1906. MacDonald was also an enthusiastic supporter of the suffrage. Finally, both Mary Neal and Emmeline Pethick were early supporters of the Council who subsequently joined with the Pankhursts.[36]

In sum, the leading members of the Council were feminists who held a broad and practical vision of feminism often imbued with the notions of women's proper place in the family accepted by the larger society. Late nineteenth- and early twentieth-century feminism was indeed often contradictory, and does not offer 'a clearly worked out ideology'.[37] The Council's activities emphasize this point. Its members were pragmatists, rather than theorists, who went out into the world to gather information about women's condition and to use the knowledge gained to improve that condition. Although they were influenced by the intellectual framework of the period as well as a commitment to a basic feminist belief, the importance of groups like the Women's Industrial Council in the history of the struggle for women's rights should not be ignored.

Notes

1 In this context, social feminists were those women who were interested in social questions affecting women's lives and who wanted to obtain economic rights for women. For the most part, they also wanted the vote but they were not going to wait for it before they demanded certain rights and a place in public life. They did not necessarily espouse socialism, although many were involved with socialist groups such as the Fabian Society. They thus saw a connection between social reform and women's rights. See also William O'Neill, *The Woman Movement* (London: George Allen & Unwin 1969), especially p. 14, for a somewhat different definition. O'Neill states that social feminists were 'those women who placed particular social reforms *ahead* of women's rights' (my italics).

2 Constance Rover, *Women's Suffrage and Party Politics in Britain 1866–1914* (London: Routledge & Kegan Paul 1967), p. 2.

3 L. Wyatt-Papworth, 'The Women's Industrial Council: A Survey', *The Women's Industrial News*, **64** (January 1914), p. 204. Hereafter *WIN*.

4 Women's Industrial Council, Seventh Annual Report, 1900–1, p. 8; and Second Annual Report, 1895–6, p. 8. Hereafter WIC.

5 Barbara Drake, *Women in Trade Unions* (London: George Allen & Unwin, n.d., *c*. 1920), p. 22; and Mary Cameron, 'Clementina Black: A Character Sketch', *The Young Woman*, **I** no. 9 (June 1983) p. 316.

6 *The Times* (London, 9 October 1899), p. 6. See also The Women's Trade Union Association, First Report (1889–90), pp. 3–4. Hereafter WTUA. See also Clementina Black, 'The Organization of Working Women', *The Fortnightly Review*, **XLVI** (November 1889), p. 704.

7 See Roger Fulford, *Votes for Women* (London: Faber & Faber 1957), p. 86 for a description of Sandhurst.

8 For information on Black see, for instance, A. Amy Bulley and Margaret Whitley, *Women's Work* (London: Methuen 1894), p. 77; *The Times* (London, 22 December 1922); Norman and Jeanne MacKenzie, *The Fabians* (New York: Simon & Schuster 1977), p. 99; and Cameron, 'Clementina Black', pp. 315–16.

9 Black, 'The Organization of Working Women', pp. 698–9.

10 On the elder Hicks see, for example, *Parliamentary Papers*, Royal Commission on Labour, 1892, **XXXV**, p. 711, C.6708–VI, Qs.8183–4; and J. Ramsey MacDonald, *Margaret Ethel MacDonald* (London: George Allen & Unwin 1912), p. 130. On Frances Hicks, see WTUA, Third Annual Report, 1891–2, p. 10, and Fourth Annual Report, 1892–3, p. 14.

11 On James, see Royal Commission on Labour, Qs.8400–1, and WTUA, Second Annual Report, 1890–1, pp. 5, 10. On Balgarnie, see Sylvia Pankhurst, *The Suffragette Movement* (London: Virago 1977, original publication 1931), p. 281.

12 WTUA, First Report, p. 9; Second Annual Report, pp. 8–9; and Third Annual Report, pp. 9–10. See also *The Times* (London, 25 January 1893), p. 11.

13 WTUA, Fourth Annual Report, pp. 4–5; Royal Commission on

Labour, Qs.8409 and 8493; and *WIN*, 8 (June 1899), p. 113.

14 *WIC*, *What the Council Is and Does* (London: Morton & Burt, Printers, January 1909), p. 1.

15 *The Times* (London, 27 November 1894), p. 12.

16 Eleanor Marx's comment is quoted in Yvonne Kapp, *Eleanor Marx*, **II**, *The Crowded Years* (London: Lawrence & Wishart 1976), p. 394. See also Clementina Black, *Sweated Industry and the Minimum Wage* (London: Duckworth & Co. 1907), pp. 135–6 and *Sussex Daily News* (21 December 1908), n.p.

17 See, for example, WIC, 'What Has Already Been Done', a leaflet found with *WIN*, 32 (September 1905), pp. 2–3, for the Council's work until 1903. See also *What the Council Is and Does*, pp. 3–4, 6, and Wyatt-Papworth, 'The Women's Industrial Council', p. 205.

18 See H. V. Toynbee's evidence given on 6 November in *Parliamentary Papers*, 1909, **XL**, p. 541, Cd.4755, Q.30622 (55), and Catherine Webb, *The Woman with the Basket* (Manchester: Co-operative Wholesale Society's Printing Works 1927), p. 111. On Black, see *Westminster Gazette* (20 September 1918), n.p., and WIC, Nineteenth Annual Report, 1912–13, p. 31.

19 *WIN*, **20** (September 1902), p. 324, and **19** (June 1902), pp. 301–2.

20 See, for example, *WIN*, 21 (December 1902), p. 342; 53 (January 1911), p. 46, and 59 (October 1912), pp. 85–6.

21 *WIN*, 15 (June 1901), pp. 242–3; and Lily H. Montagu, *My Club and I* (London: Herbert Joseph 1942), pp. 14, 69.

22 Information for the following paragraphs on the activities of the Clubs Industrial Association is found in issues of the *Women's Industrial News* which periodically carried descriptions of meetings and so on. See also Montagu, *My Club and I*, p. 65.

23 WIC, Tenth Annual Report, 1903–4, p. 24.

24 *WIN*, **15** (June 1901), p. 240, 21 (December 1902), p. 333, **26** (March 1904), p. 413.

25 Information for the following paragraphs was taken from pages 43, 46–8, 62 and 64 of the report and issues of the *Women's Industrial News*.

26 *WIN*, **80** (January 1918), pp. 1–3, **81** (April 1918), 5–8.

27 *WIN*, **31** (June 1905), p. 484.

28 *WIN*, **55** (July 1911), p. 93, **21** (December 1902), p. 339, **62** (July 1913), p. 158, **26** (March 1904), pp. 421–3, **31** (June 1905), p. 485, and **45** (December 1908), pp. 92–4.

29 *WIN*, **51** (July 1910), p. 6 and **50** (April 1910, pp. 4, 7.

30 *Parliamentary Papers* (House of Commons), 1907 (290), **VI**, p. 55, Q.2916, 18 July. Black testimony before Select Committee on Home Work.

31 From an interview with Mrs Amie Hicks, 'The Women in Hyde Park', in *The Woman's Signal* (29 March 1894), p. 212.

32 *WIN*, **43** (June 1908), p. 34.

33 Memorial to John Burns from WIC, 14 November 1907, in *WIN*, **41** (December 1907), p. 704.

34 Mrs J. R. MacDonald and Mrs Player, 'Wage-Earning Mothers', in Mrs J. R. MacDonald *et al.*, *Wage Earning Mothers* (London: Women's Labour League, n.d.), p. 15.

35 National Union of Women's Suffrage Societies, *Women's Suffrage Deputation* (London: National Union of Women's Suffrage Societies, n.d.), p. 1.

36 See *The Englishwoman's Yearbook* (1910), p. 193; Ray Strachey, *The Cause* (New York: Kennekat Press; original publication 1928, reissued 1969), p. 245; and E. Sylvia Pankhurst, *The Suffragette* (New York: Source Book Press 1970; original publication 1911), p. 61.

37 Sheila Rowbotham, *Hidden from History* (New York: Vintage Books 1976), pp. 90–1.

PART TWO

Selections

The following selections illustrate both the history and the activities of the Women's Industrial Council and its forerunner, the Women's Trade Union Association. The sources for studying the Council are diverse and range from its own annual reports, pamphlets, and quarterly News, to newspaper articles, books written by Council members and articles found in the leading periodicals of the day. The annual reports of the WTUA are also extant and excerpts from them have been included.

2 The Women's Trade Union Association

Annual reports*

Some of the aims and activities of the Women's Trade Union Association, the forerunner of the Women's Industrial Council, are illustrated in the following excerpts from the Association's Annual Reports. The conciliatory nature of its official stance on employee–employer relations can also be seen. In addition, the optimism of the first year gives way quite soon and this, in turn, leads to an attempt by 1893 to find a different form of organization to achieve economic rights for working-class women workers in London.

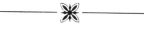

1889–90 FIRST REPORT

This Association arose out of a small meeting of friends called together by Mrs. Sheldon Amos, immediately after the dock strike last year. It was thought that the time was a particularly favourable one for some effort to improve the condition of working women, especially in the East-end. It was clear to those who wished to make this effort that the only real hope lay in combination among the workers themselves, and it was therefore resolved to form a Committee which would devote itself to founding and promoting trade unions for women, primarily in the East-end of London, but possibly in other localities as occasion should arise. The co-operation of experienced Trade Union men was especially sought, and the original Committee included four members of the London Trade Council, all officials of solid

---

* From WTUA Annual Reports, 1889–90 to 1892–3.

Trade Unions, the value of whose experience and counsel has at all times been very great. The aim of the Association has, from the first, been to establish self-managed and self-supporting Trade Unions, over which no person outside the Union should have any control whatever. The funds of the Association were intended to cover – 1st, purely propagandist expenses (hiring of halls, printing and distributing bills, &c.); 2nd, the expenses of a Central Office in the East-end; 3rd, the expense of making a temporary allowance to any woman who, in the early stages of a Union, might be dismissed solely for joining it. Such cases, it is hoped, will be few in the future as in the past; but they will be fewer the more strongly the Association is backed by public opinion, and, especially, the better its financial position. The knowledge that there is a substantial fund is essential in order to remove the fear which is the greatest hindrance to the work. 4th, any expenses that might be incurred in putting into force the laws for the protection of working women.

The subject of strikes was carefully discussed, and it was decided that no part of the Association's funds should be devoted to strike purposes. . . .

At first the Association held general meetings for working-women every Tuesday evening, in various districts, but after a time these were discontinued in favour of meetings for women in special trades.

CONFECTIONERS

The first trade organised was that of the working confectioners. A Union including men and women was formed, but was not successful, and after dwindling to a small membership was finally dissolved early in May; but was started again for women only, in July, has now a membership of about 800, and is rapidly adding fresh branches.

HAT AND CAP MAKERS

Two or three very intelligent and energetic hat and cap makers urged the Association to hold meetings for them, and two were held, but there was scarcely any attendance, and the few who came were too timid to join.

ROPEMAKERS

At one of the early general meetings some women engaged in ropemaking attended and expressed a wish to have meetings held for them. A meeting was accordingly held on the 1st of November, 1889, in the Mission Room, Dean Street, Commercial Road, kindly lent by the Rev. M. Hare. About twenty or thirty women attended from a large factory near, and showed themselves very earnest. Another meeting was held a little later; Mrs. Hicks and Miss Black went to the gates at the time of leaving work, and brought almost all the women with them to the meeting. The Union was then formally established, and Mrs. Hicks was elected Secretary.

Meetings of ropemakers were now held in the neighbourhood of the other East-end ropeworks. Women joined, and before long, men working in the trade applied to be allowed to enter the Union, and were admitted on equal terms, but after a time it was found more convenient to divide into two branches, a men's and a women's branch. This Union has been in many respects the most encouraging of all that we have founded. The intelligence, fairness, and business capacity of its members being really remarkable.

At the end of printing the Report, the ropemakers' Union is engaged in its first struggle. After nearly a year's steady work and careful inquiry into prices, the Union made a demand of Messrs. Frost Bros. for an advance which would bring their total wages up to 2d. an hour for the lowest grade, 2¼d. for the next, and 2½d. for the highest grade of work, rates which are paid by other ropemaking firms in east London for similar work. Messrs. Frost Bros. have not as yet granted these demands – which would involve about £7 a week increased expenditure – and some 100 women are at the present time out on strike.

TAILORESSES

A Union for East-end tailoresses has existed for many years, though its membership has been extremely small. The Association held several meetings for women in this trade, but passed on any tailoresses who attended them to this Union, and succeeded during the early months of its work in adding a considerable number of members.

MANTLEMAKERS

An attempt was made to organise the Mantlemakers, whose pay is bad – especially bad considering the skilled work which they do – while they suffer greatly from irregularity of employment, being some times kept very late, and at others having no work and no pay. The response from the women was, however, by no means encouraging. There is a good deal of homework in the trade, which always renders organisation difficult, and makes necessary the help of more organisers than we are able to command.

SHIRTMAKERS
Great efforts have been made to organise the East-end shirtmakers, but although we succeeded last January in establishing a Union with good prospects, its members have fallen off. We shall, however, continue to work among the shirtmakers. Experience teaches that in trades hitherto unorganised, and especially in particularly ill-paid trades, these apparently unsuccessful efforts are often a necessary prelude to successful ones.

UMBRELLA MAKERS
Meetings have been held and a Union established among women working in the umbrella-making trade. This trade is a difficult one to deal with, for two or three reasons. The factories are mostly small; there is much homework; and the hours of work are extremely uncertain and irregular. A Union is particularly necessary in order to correct this last evil, as well as to arrest the rapid decline of wages. The Association was urged to take up this work by the union of men in the same trade.

BOX MAKERS
It was again the organised men in the trade who requested the Association to try and form a union among women engaged in fancy box making. A meeting was held on the 19th of March at the Loyal United Friends' Hall, Banner Street, E.C. The attendance was small, owing largely to the very late hours often worked, but all present gave their names as members, and the Union was formally established a short time after. Meetings have been held in the districts where this work is carried on, and handbills have been largely distributed at the factories. The Union is still not large, but it has some admirable and business-like members.

BRUSH MAKERS
The youngest Union formed by the Association is that of women engaged in brushmaking, the first meeting of which was held on the 29th of July. The membership is small – other work has prevented the Association from

carrying on the meetings for various factories as promptly as could be wished – but the Union has already prevented a strike and restored amicable relations in one factory; and the master of this factory has testified, unasked, to the great improvement in punctuality brought about by the influence of the Union.

PROVINCIAL WORK

The Association has, on several occasions, been asked to help in organising women's work in the provinces, and has almost always done so. The Hon. Secretary has addressed meetings in Oxford, Cambridge, Bristol (several times), Leeds, Sheffield, Brighton, Sawston, Winsford, Portsmouth and Gloucester. In the seven last-named places the meetings have been for working women, and in the last five they have been undertaken through the action of the organised men who desired to help the women to organisation. In Brighton, the Trade Council, helped by Miss Grace Black, have organised branches of the already existing Laundresses' Union; in Winsford the Trade Council have begun to organise the local women (chiefly velveteen cutters), and an attempt will be made to carry the organisation through the trade; in Sawston the men working at paper-making have joined the Association to help in organising the women. Miss Black paid two visits, and the women nearly all enrolled themselves in a union which will be the first branch of a Trade Union of women paper-makers. In Gloucester the men of the various trade unions have made a local union for the women, who are chiefly jam and pickle makers and match makers. It is proposed that these shall affiliate themselves with the existing Unions of confectioners and of match makers. In Portsmouth the men have organised the women engaged in stay-making, and this Union too needs to be extended throughout the whole trade.

It is, we think, extremely desirable that the local organisation of women should be assisted and superintended in its early stages by a little knot of local helpers, and we are anxious to form branches of our Association in various towns and districts. Our policy here, as in London, would be the organising into one Union, consisting of many branches, that of all the women working in any special trade, so that the wages can be ascertained, a scale framed, and action be taken on a concerted plan. We feel that "general" Unions, composed of members of several distinct trades, are far less effective, and that federation must be aimed at after each trade has become fairly well organised and not before. Feeling thus, we have been careful not to bring into any Union of our own making women in whose special trade there was already a Union existing. We have referred such East-end tailoresses as we came upon to the Tailoresses' Trade Union formed by the Women's Trade Union Provident League. We have affiliated the Brighton laundresses to the Laundresses' Union, and shall try to bring about affiliation between the Gloucester Matchmakers and the matchmakers' Trade Union. We see, however, that in small places where the members of each trade are but few, there may be need for the encouraging influence of a general union, but we think this might be obtained by arranging one meeting place and meeting time, without sacrificing the more important advantage of trade amalgamation. If the women working in one trade are scattered up and down the country under the disguise of this, that or the other Workwomen's Society, or Women's Union, or Women's League, or General Federation, how is it possible that the central trade union of each particular trade can discover them, find out their wages, or induce them to accept a regular scale?

GENERAL WORK

We have, during the year, given information on several occasions to the Factory Inspectors of breaches of the law. We, in fact, have, among other instances, caused the fencing of dangerous machinery in one firm where members of one of our Unions are employed; we have called attention to the doings of a company which so flagrantly broke the law as to have rendered itself liable to a fine of over £90 for working beyond the legal hours. We are now trying to start – apart from our general fund – evening clubs for members of the Unions. The rent, firing and light would have to be covered by subscriptions from outside, while the subscriptions of the members will go towards all the other expenses, and the whole control of the club will be in the hands of the members . . . .

It is our firm conviction that organisation among women is absolutely necessary for the prevention of those frequent and futile strikes which at present occur where women and girls are employed.

Among the factories in various industries with which we have had to do in the course of the year, we have hardly met with one in which there has not been one small strike or more. The Ropemakers' and the Brushmakers'

Unions have prevented strikes among their members which would certainly have taken place if there had been no Union. The necessity of acting through the Union Committee, which sifts all grievances and acts in a formal manner, gives time for heated feelings to calm down, and restrains the hasty action of individuals. Employers, too, gain by having properly constituted representatives with whom to confer, and through whom complaints are brought to their notice in an orderly and responsible manner. They gain also, as we may proudly declare, by the general improvement in work and conduct of their workers. It is the effort of all the Unions connected with this Association to bring their members to a sense of responsibility as workers, and we have had the unasked testimony of several employers to the improved punctuality, honesty and orderliness of our Unionists. We claim that the women who join these unions not only enter upon the only path by which they may improve their miserable pay, but that they also become happier, more intelligent, more responsible; they become, in short, better workers, better women, and better citizens. . . .

1890–1 SECOND ANNUAL REPORT

Objects to which the funds of the Association are devoted:–
1.–Purely propagandist expenses (hiring of halls, printing of bills, &c.).
2.–The maintenance of a central office in the East End.
3.–Temporary allowances to any woman who, in the early stages of a Union, may be discharged solely for joining it.
4.–The defraying of any legal expenses that may be incurred in putting into force the laws for the protection of working women.

No part of the Association's funds is ever given to a Trade Union, except for definite propagandist work.

No part of the Association's funds is devoted to strike purposes.

The W.T.U.A., in completing its second year of work, cannot make a report that looks upon the surface so encouraging as last year's. The great dock strike was followed by a very remarkable wave of Trade Union feeling. All ranks of workers showed an unexampled eagerness to combine, and the founding of unions in new trades was easy. It was not to be expected that this enthusiasm would not be subject to some degree of reaction, or that the dread of their employers, which is so widespread among working women, would not reassert itself. The founders of the Association have always understood that the largest part of their work at the present stage was the spreading of a true idea of Trade Unionism – the laying of a foundation upon which true Trade Unions should arise.

The foremost aim of the Association has always been that the Unions founded by it should be genuine Trade Unions, and not either mere sick and out-of-work clubs or miscellaneous assemblages of persons belonging to all sorts of trades. . . .

The slow building up of a real trade union, with its comparatively limited but special and well-defined aims and methods, seems but a prosaic and ineffectual undertaking, and the better it is managed the less scope it affords for personal publicity. Yet this work is the work which is really needed among women wage-earners, and it is to this work that the Women's Trade Union Association has steadily devoted itself, feeling that every woman who remains a member of such a union not only advances her trade interests, but also gains as an individual a most valuable education. Unions managed from outside, or by any single person, however capable, have not this educational influence, and the Association is especially anxious that the unions founded by it should be self-controlled and self-supported. It is less troublesome, in the early stages, to manage a union than to train its members in the business of managing for themselves, but the one plan rather intensifies that lack of self-reliance which is the root of helplessness, while the other tends to cure it. . . .

In concluding this Report, the members of the Association can but urge once more upon all those who care for the interests of working women, the extreme need of putting some check upon the downward course of their already appallingly low wages. The average wage among the workers mostly dealt with this year, is less than 10s. a week, and this second year's experience leaves the Association more sadly convinced than ever that the female factory worker's life is in too many cases a life of practical slavery. The oppression, the injustice, and the grinding poverty to which a large number of working women are subject, amount to nothing less than a national disgrace, and the members of the Association are firmly resolved to help these slaves of civilisation to free themselves by means of orderly, peaceful, self-controlled combination. That the visible results of these efforts hitherto have been small is a reason, not for discouragement, but for a renewal of effort. In all fields of human advance there are seasons of rapid growth, and seasons of apparent stagnation; but the harvest that seems to spring suddenly from seeds sown long before. To sow the seeds of Trade Unionism among women is the main work of this Association.

1891–2 THIRD ANNUAL REPORT

The year just concluded has not been one of much direct progress in the work of organising either Men's or Women's Trade Unions. The favourable time for one as for the other is a rising not a falling market. It is but natural that the fluctuations of the Men's Unions, and especially of the unskilled Men's Unions, should be followed by the Women's Unions. The past year has not been one of increased membership among men, and the Women's Trade Union Association, while able to report advances in one or two quarters, cannot point to any real or general advance. In no year have more efforts been made, and in no year have the *direct* results been smaller. . . .

THE CONFECTIONER'S UNION

On the very day of the Association's last Annual Meeting, a leading member of the Confectioners' Union was discharged from her employment. She had worked for many years for the same firm, and no complaint had been made against her. The next week, other leading members of the Union were selected for dismissal, and younger sisters belonging to their families were discharged at the same time. The employer, in whose firm these dismissals took place, had promised, a year and a half earlier, not to punish or dismiss girls for belonging to the Union. It was impossible to doubt that his action was a declaration of war, and he himself did not pretend anything else. There seems reason to think that he desired to provoke a strike – the reason being one of slackness, and he having an extra stock on hand. The girls themselves were anxious to strike, but when it was presented to them that they would do harm to themselves and rather assist the employer, they wisely agreed to abstain. The employer then formally forbade all girls in his employ to belong to the Union, warned all new girls against it, and actually employed a man systematically to watch the entrance to the Girls' Union Club, held on the Association's premises. His warning of new girls was not however a very effective course, for at least one of them was led in consequence to make enquiries about the Union and to join.

Some meetings for girls in this trade held in this spring revealed appallingly low rates of payments, such as 1½d. per cwt. for folding paper packages, and ½d. per tray (of 142) for labelling packages. At this work one girl had earned 7/- in one week by working at her utmost speed. This girl must have labelled 13,856 packets for her 7/-.

In the first half of the year some meetings were again held in South London without any result whatever. In one case 3,000 handbills had been distributed, but not one woman attended.

In June, a strike arose in a large factory in South London. The women concerned had been employed to cover pots at 8d. per 100. Their employer now wished them to cover 144 for 9d.; this change, he maintained, was not a reduction, but a "readjustment." The girls, however, could not take the view that an alteration of price from covering 12½ for a penny to covering 16 for a penny was not a reduction. The strike continued for a fortnight. During the first week very young, inexperienced substitutes were put on at a weekly wage of 10/-. The work was not well done, and some orders were returned on the employer's hands. In the second week the strikers deliberately sought and found work elsewhere at better terms, the season being now busy. As they had not previously joined a Union, and therefore had no funds except what might be collected for them, this was their wisest course. They all promised to join the Confectioners' Union, a room was lent for Branch Meetings by Mr. Scott Lidgett, of the Bermondsey Wesleyan Settlement, and hopes were entertained of at last gaining some real hold on the South Side. But within a very few weeks, every member faded away from the new Branch, although Mrs. Hicks and a lady belonging to the Settlement, who had volunteered to help, made personal visits to every member. For the present therefore the same report as last year must be made of the South Side – many efforts, no result. Mrs. Hicks and Miss Black, who have devoted much time and work to this effort, are still of opinion that the work is not wasted, and that a time will yet come when the Trade Union spirit will awake in South London.

THE ROPEMAKERS' UNION

The Ropemakers' Union again largely increased its membership early in the year by the return to it of most of the Millwall workers who had fallen out. Some have since again lapsed. Efforts to gain fresh members in Stratford were not successful. The attempt will probably be renewed. A large new Branch has been formed in Canning Town, where the ladies and gentlemen of the Mansfield House Settlement have helped by lending rooms, distributing bills, assisting in secretarial work and taking part in meetings. A good many meetings were held, at all of which Mrs. Hicks was present, and at two of them Mr. Keir Hardie, M.P., spoke.

In the factory where this Union began – that of Messrs. Frost & Son – every woman belongs to the Union, and the employers are upon the friendliest terms with the Union officials and fully realise the value of organisation and cohesion among their employees. Lately, when it was desired to make some alteration in the methods of work – to which the women were at first averse – Mrs. Hicks was invited by the firm to examine all the details of the change, and having convinced herself that it was one in no way disadvantageous to the workers, called a meeting, explained the case to them, and obtained their unanimous consent to accept the alteration. This is the relation which the Association would like to see existing in every factory where women are employed – the Union serving as a medium for reasonable negotiation between employer and employed, and, while resisting all oppression on the one hand, removing on the other all unnecessary friction and misunderstanding. . . .

GENERAL WORK OF THE YEAR

The Second Annual Meeting was held at Essex Hall, on Thursday, 26th November, 1891, the late Lady Sandhurst presiding. Mr. Tom Mann, Mr. H. Tait (of the Labour Commission), Miss Black, Miss James, and the Rev. J. Mahomed, Chaplain of the London Hospital, spoke. The weather was most unfavourable, and the attendance but small.

During the year Miss Black has spoken at Liverpool, at a Congress of Lady Workers; at Kendall, to some women workers in the weaving and boot-making trades, for whom a meeting was organised by the Rev. H. V. Mills; at Cambridge, by invitation of the Ladies' Discussion Society, to a large and interested meeting; at Colchester, by invitation of the local Co-operative Society, the meeting being but small, owing to the great prevalence of influenza in the town at the time; at Tunbridge Wells, by invitation of the Women's Liberal Association; in Glasgow, by invitation of the Glasgow Women's Protective and Provident League; in Folkestone, where she was invited to address the Women's Meeting of the Church Congress; and in Manchester, where by invitation of the Women's Co-operative Guild, she read a paper upon the union between Trade Unionism and Co-operation.

In London there were several meetings held in Poplar for some tailoresses, who were dissatisfied with proposed changes in the mode of paying them. They eventually found that they did not at first lose on the new methods, and accordingly did not join a Union. Miss Hicks, Miss Black, and some members of the Amalgamated Society of Tailors, addressed these meetings.

In March Mrs. Amos, Mrs. Hicks and Miss Black were invited to address a meeting called by the Paddington Women's Liberal Federation; and in the same month the Rev. H. Price Hughes again held a Special Sunday Meeting on behalf of the Association, in which Lady Aberdeen and Miss Black took part. About £18 was collected. In May, Mrs. Hicks addressed a meeting of the Women's Liberal Federation at the Memorial Hall, and greatly impressed some of the delegates with the importance of the industrual question. In June, Mrs. Hicks and Miss Black spoke at a meeting in Battersea to inaugurate a Women's Branch of the Battersea Labour League. The General Election interfered for a time last summer with the holding of meetings, and one which had been arranged was put off.

In October, Mrs. Hicks also spoke at the Church Congress Meeting, and in November was held the large meeting reported above.

In connection with the meeting at Manchester of the Women's Co-operative Guild, the Association notes with great pleasure the disposition of several Branches to take up the work of helping to organise Women's Unions. The Battersea Branch has already held one meeting for women workers, which Miss Black attended. The members of the Women's Co-operative Guild are in many instances themselves wives of working men; they are the natural allies and helpers of women working in their districts, and the prospect of their assistance is one of the most encouraging points in the year's history.

The Factory Inspectors have again been advised of breaches of the law coming under the notice of members of the Association, and have always given prompt attention. For obvious reasons, however, the cases cannot be particularised.

In conclusion, the Association can but express the firm resolve of its members to proceed with the uphill work of organisation as long as possible, and its hope that the work will not be allowed to cease from lack of public support.

1892–3 FOURTH ANNUAL REPORT

The year just closing has been one of even greater trade depression than the last, and the discouraging conditions then noted have naturally been more, rather than less strongly marked. The organisation of workers who are paid actually below a reasonable living wage – as many women workers are – is only possible in times of unusual hopefulness, such as that which immediately followed the Dock Strike. Of course, meetings can be got up and members enrolled, but unless this attempt at organisation is very spontaneous, it may do more harm than good, and inspire in the long run rather a distrust of Trade Unionism than a faith in it. But these periods in which the active business of organisation are perforce slackened, are periods in which information can be collected, and educational work carried on. Without such previous work the Unions formed, when better times come back, are not likely to be permanent.

The conditions of the competition of women with men in the Labour Market, are among the points upon which information and education are needed by men, by women, and by the public. It is sadly true that women workers, in many instances, lack training to compete on even terms, and that they are admitted into various trades, solely because they work cheaply, to the lowering alike of men's wages, and of the general standard of work. That men should try to prevent them from doing so is neither unnatural nor reprehensible. The proper remedy, however, lies not in the exclusion of women, but in the raising alike of their skill and their wages, and in their inclusion, where possible, in men's organisations. This view, we are glad to say, is gaining ground among organised men, many of whom are among the truest friends of Women's Unions.

The better technical education of women therefore is, in many cases, almost a necessary preliminary to their effective trade organisation, and the Committee of the Association consider that the time occupied by the Secretary in her work, as a member of the London Board of Technical Education, has been time spent in the long run, for the advancement of the Association's purposes.

Voluntary association is by no means able to remedy all the evils of industrial life, and the legislature recognising this has framed various laws for the protection of various classes of workers. The Factory Inspectors appointed to enforce these laws are far too few in number, and their efforts are continually hindered by the ignorance and timidity of the workers concerned.

A knowledge of the Factory and Workshops' Act, the Truck Act, the Shop Hours' Act, and the Employers' Liability Act, should be possible for every workman and workwoman, and until such knowledge becomes part of the ordinary course of education, it is the business of such bodies as the Association, to try and fill the gap. More knowledge, too, is needed of the circumstances of special trades, in order both to procure legislation when particular conditions require it, and to prevent legislation where it would place women at an unfair disadvantage.

Finally, much more knowledge of the conditions of women's work is needed by the public at large. Many of the evils now existing could not possibly continue if public opinion were fully awake to their occurrence. Moreover, for the present, the work of promoting women's organisations needs to be supported by contributions from the public, and these contributions can only be obtained by waking the public to a comprehension of the real needs of working women, and the real nature of trade organisation. Even this year of depression more might have been done if the Association had not been crippled by want of funds.

ROPEMAKERS' TRADE UNION

Again, a very satisfactory report may be given of this Union. The membership continues firm and steady, while its benefits to the workers have been again demonstrated by the easy settlement of what might have been a serious dispute. This time the women in a large factory were requested to oil their own machinery, in order to save the wages of the man who had previously had that duty to perform. The women unanimously refused to do this on account of the danger to themselves; while the machinery was in motion, their loose clothing could easily get caught and injuries result, which could not be compensated. At the request of the employer, Mrs. Hicks, the Secretary of the Union, was sent for, and after a few hours' consultation, the difficulty was arranged on satisfactory terms to both parties, and without the loss of even a day's work.

During the summer a day's excursion was planned by the Union for the women of this firm; it was the first of the kind that had taken place, and proved very satisfactory. Epping was the place chosen, and as the weather was fine, the outing was greatly enjoyed. The employer and other friends contributed towards the expenses.

The branch of the Mat and Fibre workers at Canning Town, which last year joined the Ropemakers' Union, during this year has separated and formed another Union, in the hope of ultimately being amalgamated with the Men's Union of the same trade.

THE ROPEMAKERS' TRADE UNION CLUB

Although this Club now takes the name of the Union to which most of its members belong, it is in reality a continuation of the Club that has existed now for three years. The funds that supplied rent, firing and lighting, were almost exhausted, and Rev. H. Henman, of St. Mary's, Shadwell, kindly offered the use of his school-room, at Johnson Street, free of charge for one night a week. Every Friday evening is now devoted to the members who busily enjoy themselves with Physical Drill (of which they have given one exhibition), needlework, singing, dancing, and Trade Union work. If funds for utensils are forthcoming, it is intended to arrange cookery and other domestic classes.

CONFECTIONERS' UNION

This Union, which has had a very brilliant and eventful career, has been obliged to dissolve its membership. The marked opposition of the employees was no doubt a contributory cause of this failure, but we believe it to be chiefly due to the present condition of the trade itself. Juvenile labour, which has always been employed to a considerable extent, has very much increased during the last year or so, and it will be easily understood that juvenile labour does not lend itself to permanent organisation. Where a succession of young girls is constantly passing through a factory, there can be no real coherence, and only the influence of some strong personality can hold them together. At the same time, it must not be supposed that, when special occasion arises it is not worth while to form a Trade Union among workers of this kind. Such a Union can often obtain the remedy of a specific grievance, and is, under all circumstances, an educating influence. Girls who have belonged to the Confectioners' Union have gained an understanding of Trade Union principles and a wider view of labour questions than could probably have been given them in any other way, and wherever they may go they become, often unconsciously, centres of Trade Union influence. In short, the Union has done good work, and in special similar cases, the same work could be, and probably will, sooner or later, be repeated. . . .

FACTORY LEGISLATION

At the time of the last Report, there was a growing agitation, in which the Association had been particularly active, in favour of increased inspection and of the' appointment of women inspectors. On Jan. 24th the Home Secretary received a deputation on the subject, numbering some hundreds of delegates. Among the societies represented were the Trade Union Congress, World's Women's Temperance Union, Women's Liberal Federation, Women's Trade Union League, Women's Provident and Protective League, Glasgow, and the Women's Trade Union Association.

Miss Balgarnie, Mrs. Hicks, Miss James, Miss Simmons, and Miss Cameron were the appointed delegates on behalf of the Association.

The Home Secretary expressed his approval of Women Inspectors, and subsequently appointed two, as well as fifteen additional Working Men Inspectors.

Experience, however, has shown the Association that whatever increase of Factory Inspectorship might be made, the ignorance regarding the Acts existing among the workers, must always remain a serious obstacle to efficient inspection. It was felt that before leaving school, young people should be instructed in the protection accorded to them by law; therefore a letter was drafted and sent to Mr. Acland, Minister of Education, stating our desire that in all Elementary Schools under Government inspection, instruction in such industrial legislation as the Factory and Workshop's Act, Employers' Liability Act, Shop Hours' Act, Mines' Act, &c., should be given to boys and girls of the Higher Standards, including information on the hours of employment, overtime, deductions from wages, accidents, &c.

Arguments and instances illustrating the necessity of such instruction were given for the consideration of Mr. Acland.

A similar resolution was proposed by Miss Hicks, and carried unanimously at the London Trades' Council, which further asked Mr. Acland to provide a text book supplying the necessary information. Mr. Acland replied in both cases that he would give the subject his careful consideration; but that it was not in his power to provide text books. At the recent Tailors' Conference in Birmingham the same request was repeated.

Meanwhile, as part of our work, Miss Hicks has prepared a lecture explaining the provisions of the Factory and Workshop's Act, especially intended for girls and working women. This was delivered for the first time to a large meeting of Jewish tailoresses in Whitechapel. Since then it has been frequently given, notably to a large meeting of factory workers, called by the Women's Co-operative Guild at Tamworth, a combined meeting of several Branches of the Guild at Birmingham, and also at a Sectional Conference of the Guild, held at the Wholesale Co-operative Society, Leman Street. Everywhere it is much appreciated, and a good deal of the knowledge seems to come quite new. Numbers of other meetings, both at Girls' Clubs and Guild Branches, are being arranged. . . .

The chocolate-makers' strike

This article by Clementina Black, 'The Chocolate-Makers' Strike', appeared in *The Fortnightly Review* in August of 1890.* It describes the involvement of the WTUA with girls in the confectionary trade during a ten-day period and shows even though the Association officially decried the use of its funds to aid strikes, the Association's members still gave advice and personal support to workers on strike.

---

* This article originally appeared in *The Fortnightly Review*, XLVII (August 1890), pp. 305–14.

THE last three weeks have witnessed a fresh phase of that uprising of labour in the East End of which the match-girls' strike was the first, and the dockers' strike the second act. Three weeks ago, if the members of the Women's Trade Union Association, which has worked steadily for nine months at the organization of women workers in the East End, were to have been asked, "What is your greatest failure?" "Where have you least hope?" they must have answered, "Among the confectioners." To-day it is precisely the confectioners who give us the greatest encouragement, and who have already done more than any women in London since the match-girls to help forward the whole movement for bettering the conditions of working women. I think that a brief account of the ten days' struggle from one who saw every incident of it may be of some interest, and even of some instruction, to readers who have not the opportunity of seeing and knowing for themselves what sort of person the East End factory girl really is, and still less of understanding the inner or working side of a strike.

The first seeds of the growth which seemed to break forth so suddenly this summer were sown last autumn, when a member of the Women's Trade Union Association was informed that the men working at Messrs. Allen's were dissatisfied with their conditions, and that some of them were meditating a strike. The rules of the firm were laid before him, and appeared to him to justify complaint. He advised the men, however, not to strike, but to form a trade-union. Meetings were held, and were numerously and enthusiastically attended. A union was formed, which included both men and women, and in its first few weeks it numbered about three hundred members. How it happened that a union, starting with such a membership, and having the assistance as honorary secretary of a lady of considerable trade-union experience, should have dwindled away in about six months to nothing, is a question into which it is needless to enter. Probably, however, the main reason was to be found in a lack of trade-union knowledge and spirit among those who joined. Early in May this languishing union met and formally dissolved. At that meeting a hope was expressed that another might shortly be formed, for women only; and the dissolution had not taken place a week before regrets for having let it fail, came in from girls in the trade. Meetings were accordingly again held by the Trade Union Association, and were attended as a general thing by about three girls. These few promised to be eager disciples, but were hopeless about getting their comrades to join. "Oh yes, it would be the best thing." "Ah, but some of 'em won't ever join." "They are afraid they will be sacked." "They are so selfish; they don't care so long as they get their money for themselves." These are the sort of remarks with which the confectioners responded to our praises of trade-unionism. On Thursday, the 10th of July, a little meeting for the girls in Messrs. Allen's factory was held. Twelve girls came, and their dread of being followed, watched, and subsequently discharged, was pitiful. They did, however, all join, and promised to try and bring in others. On the next evening, Friday, 11th July, Miss James, who has herself worked in the confectionery trade, but is now employed as an organizer by the Women's Trade Union Association, went down to Messrs. Allen's factory to distribute handbills explaining the objects of the Union. To her amazement she found the girls standing about in a crowd, though it was not yet seven o'clock. They surrounded her, telling her that they were "out", and asking anxiously, "What shall we do?" "Is there anybody who will help us?" Miss James led them to the office of the Women's Trade Union Association, 128, Mile End Road, where I happened to be. She hurried in, exclaiming: "Allen's girls are out on strike – and they are here." They were there, indeed. In a twinkling the room was full and over-full of girls, and the street outside was full of those girls who could not come in, and of the fringe of on-lookers which gathers so speedily in that great boulevard of the East End, the Mile End Road. Miss James and I said a word or two to the whole company, promising to go into the matter very carefully, and to do all that could be done for them, and urged upon them the duty of orderly behaviour. Six were then chosen to stay and tell their tale, which they did in the most direct and admirable way. A girl, whom we may call X. Y., had slipped down on Thursday, and the others had laughed. The forewoman had asked who was making the disturbance. X. Y. answered, explaining, and was told that she would be fined. "Then I shan't pay my hospital penny," said X. Y. She was bidden not to be impertinent, and replied that she was not impertinent. There for that night the matter ended. Next morning she was summoned to the office, and was informed that she had the choice of being fined or dismissed. She understood that the fine, including one for a previous trivial offence, would be half-a-crown. She returned to her work, and the other girls in her department refused to go on working until she should be reinstated. This occurred in the morning, and no work was done all day. After five in the afternoon Mr. Allen himself came up and inquired why they were not working. One of them replied that they wanted an explanation of the punishment of X. Y. Their master told them to put on their hats and go home. They did so, and the dispute thus took the shape of a lock out.

This tale was told with perfect simplicity and straightforwardness; it was impossible not to believe in its substantial accuracy. Then came the other grievances. They were not allowed to leave the factory in the dinner hour; they were forbidden to eat any food between eight and one on week days or eight and two on Saturdays; they were liable to vexatious fines and deductions. We told them that a meeting would be held at three the next afternoon, that meanwhile every girl was to apply in the usual way for her week's payment, and that X. Y. was on no account to accept her money with the fine taken out of it. The next step was to telegraph to Mr. John Burns to come to the meeting, which was held at the Mile End Liberal and Radical Club in Globe Road, on Saturday. None but girls from Messrs. Allen's various factories were admitted. Questions were put to them and answered with care and moderation. Then a committee was elected from among themselves and a register taken of the names, ages, and wages of all present, every one of whom, I may say, gave in her name to join the trade-union. This meeting was our first opportunity of seeing the girls *en masse*, and the points, which no observer could have failed to notice, were the high average of good looks and the prevailing pallor and langour. The general prettiness of all but the very roughest of working girls is indeed always noticeable when a number of them are gathered together. Comparing these with the girls of the Ropemakers' Union, who work chiefly in the open air or open sheds, and who are conspicuous for their look of robust health, one felt that the need of an extra hour or so of air out of doors was indeed real. We found that all had received their week's money, and that no attempt had been made to impose the threatened fine on X. Y. The wages stated by the girls were confirmed by a number of their pay-slips which we still have, which show that fines were in truth frequent.

Next morning Mr. Burns and Miss James were at the factory considerably before eight-o'clock, the hour of going in to work. On my own arrival somewhat later I found a business-like system of picketing already established, and learned that about thirty workers had gone to work on Saturday, most of them actuated by a fear that their wages would otherwise be kept back, while only eight were at work on the Monday morning. Perfect order prevailed. A detachment of police was on the scene, having been summoned, we were assured, by an alarming description of broken heads and broken windows. The factory with its pale brick wall, blue name-plates, and many windows (not a broken pane among them), stood facing us, presenting a view that was to become very familiar as the days went on. The workpeople's entrance was open; from time to time a clerk would peep out. A cart full of packing-cases was being unloaded at the gate. The girls stood about in little knots, looking for the most part pale and anxious, and a fringe of small boys, constantly dispersed, but quickly re-assembling, hung on the heels of Mr. Burns, and stood round to listen every time he paused to speak to a policeman or a girl.

The first step was to secure a committee-room close at hand. After a good deal of fruitless inquiry, a room in Skidmore Street was offered to us, at considerable inconvenience to herself, by the wife of a member of the Dockers' Union. Like nearly all the wives of the East End, she regarded Mr. Burns as a personal benefactor, and her gratitude took the shape of eager watchfulness over the needs of the whole staff, and a constant readiness to provide them with meals. To this care, perhaps, rather than to the superlative virtue of these agitators themselves, may be attributed the really remarkable good temper which prevailed in the committee-room. The *personnel* consisted mainly of four persons – Mr. Burns, Miss Simmons (secretary of the Women's Trade Union Association), Miss James (secretary of the Confectioners' Trade Union) and the writer of these pages. Our first business was to send a polite note to Mr. Allen, the head of the firm, telling him that the girls lately employed in his chocolate works had applied to us for advice and help, and asking him to allow us to call and see him. The next point was to obtain money for the support of the eighty or ninety girls who had put themselves under our guardianship. We drew up a brief appeal, and dispatched it to the printer. We sent off girls to various trade unions and clubs in search of collecting-boxes. A note had appeared in several of the morning papers, and subscriptions were already coming to us. The rules of the Women's Trade Union Association expressly forbid the application of any part of its funds to the support of a strike, but we well knew that we could reckon upon many of the London and provincial trade unions to support us. We held a little debate as to our methods of relief. By one o'clock or so the girls began to show signs of depression, although not of timidity. "Oh, no; Mr. Samuel will never give in," they began to say; and then a rumour ran round that Mr. Allen had declared he would close his factory for three months, or altogether. We pointed out to them that no man who spends large sums upon building a factory and laying in expensive machinery is likely to be so idiotic as to waste his outlay in a fit of ill-temper against his work girls – particularly when they ask him for no advance of wages. We also pointed out that if Mr. Allen did close his factory, the only result would be that the chocolate now made there would be made in some other factory, and that the girls to make it would still be wanted. But though they saw these points they remained a little sad. It was not that they desired to go in to work; on the contrary their views of the discomforts and grievances of their life in the factory looked to them even darker than in the morning. The malady was clear; they wanted a meal. We had already money enough for that, and we decided that there could be no better way of spending it and no more effectual form of relief than to arrange for a meal for every one of them. Mr. Burns went off to negotiate with a neighbouring coffee-room proprietor, and I proceeded to write out a ticket for every girl on the register, entitling her to a fourpenny tea. When these preparations were finished, the girls were called together and Mr. Burns announced the scheme and distributed the tickets. The faces of the girls were enough. We had found the proper treatment. Next day, when funds poured in, we printed lunch tickets representing 1½d., and tea tickets in the form of a double twopenny ticket, one of which entitled to tea and bread and butter, the other to any sort of food. These we continued from that time onward, and are convinced that relief in this form given daily, is more valuable and acceptable than the corresponding number of shillings at the week's end. 5½d. may seem but a scanty allowance, but 5½d. goes further in the East End than the West, and it is certainly a fact that the girls looked better in health during every day that they were out.

As seven o'clock drew near, a considerable crowd began to assemble, and the small boys who naturally revel in any disturbance were excessively troublesome. The girls working in the other two factories of the firm (Canal Road and Copperfield Road) joined themselves to the crowd, which became more and more vociferous as the minutes went on and the workpeople still did not appear. We, for our parts, stood close to the door, doing what we could to help the police in keeping a clear path. At last the door opened and the men employed came out. Two unpopular officials were a little hooted, but the main demonstration was reserved until later. One could not help being irresistibly reminded of a crowd at some entertainment whose eagerness is heightened by delay, and who receive with a sort of impatience the minor persons of the stage. The seven girls came next, and last of all the forewoman, to whom, rightly or wrongly, the girls and the people of the neighbourhood attribute the greater part of the discomfort experienced by those who worked under her. The crowd hooted her, though I think few of the girls joined in that chorus; and a rush was made to follow the little procession as the door closed on them. For the moment there was a good deal of pushing, hustling, and shouting, and there seemed a possibility of girls getting knocked down and hurt. Nothing of the sort, however, took place, and there was never any likelihood of anything more serious. With this demonstration Monday's proceedings closed. We had painted our appeals, arranged our commissariat and our picketing, applied to the employer for an interview, held a private meeting of the committee, at which we drew up a statement of demands, and two open-air meetings in a street-end where there was no thoroughfare. We had found out that the girls with whom we had to deal were an orderly, capable, and self-respecting little community, and we had also found out that there were disadvantages as well as advantages in having for leader a man whose face and name are known in every East End street, and who is "shadowed" by a persistent concourse of persons anxious to miss no opportunity of hearing him speak. To walk through the East-End with Mr. Burns is to hear him greeted by name by at least half the men, women, and children whom one meets; every policeman has a smile and a salute for him, and the only persons with whom he is unpopular are, so far as I saw, the publicans, whom I have heard curse him from their doorways as he passed. If he were indeed the violent revolutionary for whom the country readers of one or two newspapers still take him, he might have an army at his back to-morrow. Indeed, he has that army – or perhaps I should say that congregation – already, and he preaches to it continually the doctrines of cleanliness, sobriety, and organization.

On Tuesday morning, when we arrived at eight o'clock, we found that the girls from the Canal Road and Copperfield Road factories had not gone in to work and wanted to join the strike. These factories were not making chocolate, and therefore were not doing the work of those who were "out."

It was not therefore necessary for our success that they should cease work, and we perceived that our position would be more strengthened by having them inside, but ready to be withdrawn at any moment, than by adding them to those who were out already. Apart from this, we had no desire to cause loss or inconvenience unnecessarily to Mr. Allen or his customers. Mr. Burns therefore exhorted, and indeed almost compelled, them to go in at the half-hour, promising that all should be called out if this were found necessary. To my own mind this seems an even greater triumph than our final success. To bring a group of dissatisfied workers away from their work is easy enough; to induce them, against their wishes, to return to it and go on quietly while others fight the battle, is a real moral victory.

Into the Emmott Street factory no woman went that day, except the forewoman; and three girls, who were coming to apply for work, turned back when the pickets told them the state of things. The pickets had no bad time of it, for the neighbours, who strongly sympathised, brought out seats for them, and illustrated papers were provided. They sat at ease reading in the sunshine, and the police, whose attitude was of the friendliest, strolled up and down or stood talking with them. It is my own impression that the police at any rate felt some regret when this state of things came to an end. From that day everything was smooth and organized. But let no one suppose that smoothness or organization can be secured without hard work. This strike has meant sixteen to eighteen hours' work daily for the "agitators" who have been managing it. Every day there were boxes to open, to screw up, to label, and to distribute to the collectors; every day there were some £7 worth of copper to be counted and packed in rolls of 5s., and only those who have counted East-end coppers gathered on a wet day know the unpleasantness of that task. All day long subscriptions kept coming, receipts had to be sent, all money got or spent had to be entered, there were subscription lists to be made out and sent to newspapers, and visitors and reporters had to be received and dealt with civilly, however inconvenient their appearance at the particular moment. Never shall I forget the stupefaction with which the French visitor brought by M. de Blowitz contemplated the entries in our ledger. The bag of working men's pennies, too heavy to be lifted, amazed them greatly, but the West-end subscriptions amazed them even more. A letter lay waiting for Mr. Burns with the House of Commons imprint on the envelope; he came in and opened it, showing it them. "Ah, d'un Depute!"

exclaimed these gentlemen. "Rien dedans," said one nodding sagely. But there was something in it; it was a donation of £5. Then they went outside and saw the policemen greet Mr. Burns and heard them ask how things were going. I believe they thought England a strange Gilbert-and-Sullivan land of topsy-turveydom. . . .

On Wednesday, Mr. Burns received an answer from Mr. Allen, politely declining any mediation, and saying that he would rather deal with his workpeople direct. On this, a deputation of girls was elected, and a letter sent in, asking Mr. Allen to see them. The following demands were resolved on. That the girl whom I have called X. Y. should be reinstated. That the girls should be allowed to go out or stay in as they pleased in the dinner hour. That an interval should be allowed for lunch. That all fines should be abolished. That if a girl absented herself for a day, she should not be sent home again for the next day or two or three days, afterwards. That no girls should be punished or dismissed for joining a trade union, or for taking part "in the present movement." A demand was also made for the removal of the forewoman, but that was regarded rather as a form of warning and protest than as a measure to be insisted on. On Thursday came two letters from Mr. Allen – one to the girls appointing a time to see them, one to Mr. Burns asking for an unofficial interview. Mr. Burns went over in the afternoon, and spent three hours in conversation of a perfectly amicable character with Mr. Allen. Perhaps it would not be strictly in order to report what occurred at this interview, since Mr. Allen so definitely bargained for its being "unofficial." It is enough to say that from that time forward Mr. Burns, Miss Simmons, Miss James, and myself felt no serious doubts about the termination of the dispute at an early date. The deputation went in next morning, and after that there were two more meetings between Mr. Allen and his workpeople, including on one occasion sundry men – who do not seem to have been chosen by their comrades to represent them, and who expressed a desire for the retention of late fines which is entirely repudiated by many of their mates – one meeting between Mr. Allen and Mr. Burns, and two meetings between Mr. Allen, Mr. Burns, and myself. The points over which difficulties arose were the going out to dinner, which was finally granted in a form which suited the girls, and the imposition of fines. The girls may go out, if they wish to do so, either at 1 o'clock, or at 1.30, returning in either case at 2. A girl who lives near can thus go home for the whole hour; while a girl who lives at a distance can eat her dinner in the dining-room of the factory, and then go out for the rest of her time. As to the fines, Mr. Allen consented readily to abolish all except those for coming late, and these he largely reduced. It is our belief that the whole system of "late" fines is a mistaken one, and actually encourages unpunctuality by making a man or woman reflect, "I pay for being late, and so I have a right to be, if I choose." It is better that a few chronic offenders should be discharged in the course of the year than that this little vexatious – and ineffectual – tax should be levied on all. The final compromise was accepted on the following grounds. Mr. Allen assured us that all fines went towards the yearly payment to an insurance society, which would compensate all his workers in case of accident. The girls are not very likely to need this compensation, but the men are more or less liable to accidental injury; hence the desire of some of them that the girls should continue to be fined in order to provide the insurance fund. We maintain that the retention of fines on any such grounds as this – unless, indeed, the girls desired the retention, which they emphatically do not – is unjustifiable. As, however, Mr. Allen has already made his arrangements with the insurance company for the current year, the girls were willing that the "late" fines, in their reduced form, should continue until December 31st. Mr. Allen has promised that he will then make other insurance arrangements, with the consent of his employees, and will abolish the fines altogether. He does, however, make this promise conditional upon the attendance of the girls not showing a marked falling-off between this and December. On that point we feel no doubt. The girls themselves fully realise the importance of acting loyally towards their employer, and showing that he rather gains than loses by giving them better conditions. The letter containing these conditions was finally signed by Mr. Allen, Mr. Burns, and myself on Wednesday, 22nd July, and we parted from Mr. Allen on the friendliest terms, with an invitation from him to come and visit the factory when we choose, and to come and see the girls at work. From Mr. Allen we went straight to Messrs. Callard and Bowser, at whose butter-scotch works some of the girls had come out on strike, and had appealed to us. These gentlemen also received us in the most amicable manner. They had already granted an advance of wages, and they had never imposed fines. The other changes, *i.e.*, leave to come out in the dinner hour, and an interval for lunch, they granted readily, and expressed, not only to us, but to the girls themselves at a meeting the same evening, their perfect willingness that the girls should join the union, which they are doing.

To sum up these hasty and, I fear, somewhat disconnected notes, I should like to say a word or two of warning. Here are two cases in which the girls have virtually got all they want by striking. Mr. Burns, Miss Simmons, Miss James, and myself have taken up their cause and carried it through for them; but we have known that the way chosen, not by us, but by them, was not the best way. We would rather have seen a strong union which could make application to the employer in the first instance through the properly elected representatives of the girls themselves. If the union had been strong there need probably have been no leaving off work at Messrs. Allen's, and certainly no strike at Messrs. Callard's. Let no light-hearted enthusiasts deceive themselves with the idea that because these strikes have succeeded it is always easy to succeed, or that because on this occasion – chiefly through their confidence in Mr. Burns – workmen, peers, members of Parliament and County Councillors have subscribed between £200 and £300 in less than a fortnight, therefore the public may always be trusted to find support for any number of girls. Least of all, let them suppose that a strike can be carried out successfully without a staff of at least two or three really business-like persons who are willing – and able – to work night and day if need be. . . .

CLEMENTINA BLACK

3 The Women's Industrial Council

Inaugural meeting, 26 November 1984

The following selection is from *The Times* (1894),* and highlights the key speeches made at a conference called by the WTUA, at which time the Women's Industrial Council came into being. One of the speakers, R. B. Haldane, became the first president of the Council. He was succeeded by the liberal Lady Aberdeen during the year 1897–8.

WTUA CONFERENCE

At the invitation of the Women's Trade Union Association, a conference was held yesterday at the Holborn Town Hall to take into consideration women's labour in the metropolis and the desirability of forming a central council to undertake systematic inquiry into the conditions of this work and wages. There were a large number of delegates present, representing over 100 societies.

Sir J. Hutton (Chairman of the LCC), who presided at the morning sitting, congratulated the meeting on the fact that it had at last been determined to make a definite effort on behalf of the working women of London. . . .

The report of the WTUA showed the helpless condition in which the women workers of London were. It was an indictment of some of the trades of London, charging long hours, insufficient times for meals, low wages, and inadequate sanitary arrangements. What they said was that it was impossible

---

* This selection is from *The Times* (Tuesday, 27 November 1894), p. 12.

to go on as they were now, and that was their answer to those who said legislative interference was impossible. (Cheers) They wanted a simple, clear, and precise measure which would commend itself to the mind and conscience of every reasonable man and woman. There were good employers in the metropolis, but there were those whose greed knew no bounds, and if it were too herculean a task to wipe away the tears from all eyes, they might at 'least eradicate some of the terrible status that today disgraced our streets and dishonoured our civilization.' (Cheers)

Miss C. Black then moved the following resolution, which was seconded by Miss Irwin, secretary of the Scotch council, and after discussion, carried by a large majority:– 'That in the opinion of this conference it is desirable that a central council shall be established to organize special and systematic inquiry into the conditions of working women, to provide accurate information concerning those interests, and to promote such action as may seem conducive to their improvement.'

At the afternoon sitting the chair was occupied by Canon Scott-Holland, when a resolution appointing various committees to the proposed council was considered and carried. Amongst these were an investigation committee to obtain and schedule information concerning the condition of women's employment, an organization committee to assist and promote trade organizations, technical and other classes, and social clubs, and a Parliamentary & Legal Committee to watch Parliamentary proceedings, to note special and test cases in the law Courts, and to promote such legislative action as the central council may consider desirable.

At the evening meeting Mr. R. B. Haldane, Q.C. M.P., who presided, said it had been observed that London was apathetic and did not respond to popular movements; but he felt sure that the great City would not be apathetic to the movement inaugurated that day, which affected nearly a million women workers in the metropolis. They desired to raise substantially the conditions of industrial working women, not only as far as hours of work and wages went, but to improve the tone assumed by employers towards those who eventually live by the sweat of the brow. It was nothing short of a scandal that women should receive such wages as they did for shirt-making in the East-End of London, compared with the remuneration that went to those who, through the accidents of fortune, were born to such a state as secured them a good education. (Cheers) They were hoping to make it possible that in the future women should obtain a more adequate share in the returns from their own productive activity than had been the case in the past.

Before the conferences closed a resolution was carried pledging the meeting to support the central council in every way.

What the Council Is and Does

Over the years, the Council published summaries of its activities. One such summary was entitled *What the Council Is and Does*, and appeared in January 1909.* It is interesting because it details the work of the various Council committees. At the time it was issued, Clementina Black was President of the Council.

THE Women's Industrial Council has been in existence since 1894, when it grew out of the Women's Trade Union Association, which since the Great Dock Strike of 1889 had been doing valiant service in the East End of London. The preliminary work carried on during those years shewed how desirable it was to establish permanently and on a broader basis as an association whose aim it should be to watch over the interests of women engaged in trades, and over all industrial matters which concern women. That is what the Council was formed to do, and it has confined itself to this its special duty; and in order to avoid all overlapping it has put many tempting opportunities from it, and avoided all overlapping with other Societies which deal with the interests of professional women, of the poor as such, and of children, except in so far as they are engaged in trades.

Thus the object of the W.I.C. may be briefly summarised as being the improvement of all industrial conditions, whether general or special, in which women are concerned. To attain this object, the Council has to be

---

* The Women's Industrial Council, *What the Council Is and Does* (London: Morton & Burt, Printers, January 1909).

continuously alert and active in ways of which the following are the most important. It has –

1. To investigate the actual facts of women's work, and collect and publish trustworthy information about the conditions of their employment.

2. To scrutinise Parliamentary Bills, Official Reports, and legal and statistical matter of various kinds, as they bear upon the industrial interests of women; and to promote such petitions and deputations as may seem desirable in connection with legislation or local government.

3. To report, after due enquiry, to the proper authorities, breaches of the Factory and Public Health Acts.

4. To act as Poor Women's Lawyer, through the Hon. Consulting Solicitor, Mr. R. S. Garnett, in giving advice, and also in the conduct of approved cases in the Courts.

5. To educate industrial workers in social questions, economics and legislation affecting their trades or interests, through newspaper and citizenship classes, lectures and conferences, and by meeting them in their clubs and elsewhere, to learn their views and needs.

6. To find for societies and institutions efficient lecturers on subjects of social and industrial interest.

7. To publish leaflets and pamphlets on such subjects, and a quarterly organ, *The Women's Industrial News.*

8. To bring and keep before the public and the authorities the needs of unemployed women dependent on their own earnings, and to make suggestions towards the solution of the problem.

9. To promote by all means in its power the recognition of the need of girls to receive technical and trade training, either in trade schools or by some form of apprenticeship, and to see that the needs of girls receive attention proportionate to that bestowed on boys.

10. To promote the training of girls of the industrial classes as children's nurses, both with a view to providing an opening for remunerative work and to fitting them for their future lives as wives and mothers.

The Council consists of a considerable number of persons living in different parts of the country and engaged in every variety of social work. It is wholly unsectarian and independent of party. It has therefore a wide connection and varied experience upon which to draw. New members are admitted by election on the nomination of two members, and the subscription is left to the generosity of members, with a minimum of one shilling, in order that no one may be deterred from joining for financial reasons. A very large number of persons subscribe to the Council without actually becoming members. Membership gives the right to attend the Council Meetings, which are held three times a year, and to move and vote on resolutions, and otherwise to influence corporate action. The Council is on important questions its own executive, though ordinary business is entrusted to an Executive Committee and to the three standing Committees, the Investigation, the Education and the Legal.

It is impossible here even to outline the work done by the Council, but a few of the salient features in the recent work of each of the Committees, together with the business now on hand, are given below. Further enquiries are invited, and a copy of the Annual Report and of the Council's quarterly magazine, the Women's Industrial News (price 2/- per annum, post free), will be sent free on application.

THE INVESTIGATION COMMITTEE

1. The work of the Investigation Committee forms the basis for all the rest, for nothing at the present day needs such patient, accurate examination as labour questions, and of all such questions none are more difficult to understand and to deal with than those which affect women. In this lies the *raison d'être* of the council, for without full investigation it is impossible either to legislate or to organise wisely. This Committee, strengthened by volunteers drawn from the Settlements and elsewhere, undertakes from time to time to investigate the actual conditions in one of its chief centres of a given trade in which women are employed. This means visitation, with systematised enquiry of employers, factories, workshops, home-workers, employees, trade union and other officials, and then the drawing up of a report, with tabulations. The record of this work has been published in *Home Industries of Women in London: with an account of the development and present conditions of Home Work in relation to the Legal Protection of the Workers, and some Account of foreign experiments in legislation* (price 9d., post free). This Report has just been brought up to date and issued for the third time. Reports of trades investigated have appeared from time to time in the *19th Century, the Economic Journal*

and the *Women's Industrial News*. A full list will be found in the *Annual Report*. Those investigated during recent years include *Laundry Work, Jewellery,* and *Jewel Case making*, *Millinery and Artificial Flower making, Embroidery, Machining and Tailoring* (price 6d. each, post free). At the request of a Committee of the Economic Section of the British Association, the Council furnished a report on the effect of legislation on women's labour in the Tailoring trade. It remains to mention the monumental work on *Women in the Printing Trades*, edited by Mr. J. Ramsay Macdonald, M.P., for a special Committee, on which the Royal Economic Society and Royal Statistical Society were represented. All the information collected during the course of investigation is placed at the service of the Apprenticeship and Skilled Employment Association and its affiliated societies, the W.I.C. being partly responsible for its foundation. At the present moment the Committee is busy with an enquiry into the effects, economic and hygienic, of the industrial work of married women. This enquiry is being pushed forward in the provinces as well as in London, and it is hoped that the results when published will be of great use in many directions. Offers of help and special donations towards the heavy expenses inevitable in connection with this enquiry are urgently needed.

Chairman — Miss Clementina Black.
Hon. Sec. — Mrs. Bernard Player.

THE EDUCATION COMMITTEE

The Education Committee had, under the late Mrs. F. G. Hogg, the important task of initiating the whole enquiry into the work for wages of school children. The question was first investigated by members of the Council under Mrs. Hogg's direction, and the results were published by her in the *Nineteenth Century*. Her article attracted great attention; Sir John Gorst made an enquiry amongst teachers and managers in public schools and the outcome was an Interdepartmental Committee on the Employment of School Children. Much evidence was taken and a Bill drafted, which has now become law. The Committee on Wage Earning Children (Hon. Sec. Miss Adler, 6, Craven Hill, W.) was formed by the W.I.C. and the N.U.W.W. to specialise on the work.

It was also largely owing to the repeated representations made by the

Council that the L.C.C. appointed a Special Committee of the Technical Education Board to enquire into the technical education provided for girls, and it was in accordance with the evidence given by the Council that in September, 1904, a day trade school for waistcoat making was opened at the Borough Polytechnic. The school has a two years' course, 22 hours a week are devoted to trade training under an experienced trade teacher, the rest of the time is spent in general education, drawing and physical exercises. Since that date other schools in similar lines in dressmaking, ladies' tailoring, the designing and making of ready-made clothing, corset making, upholstery, and laundry work have been opened through the instrumentality of the late Mrs. Oakeshott, at the Borough and Woolwich Polytechnics, the Shoreditch and Paddington Technical Institutes and the Westminster Institute. A National Conference on the Industrial Training of Women and Girls was held by the W.I.C. at the Guildhall on October 6th, 1908. The morning session was devoted to the discussion of day trade schools for girls, and it is hoped that the result will be an increase in the number of such schools for girls in London, and that similar schools will soon be started in other big towns in various parts of the country.

The Committee is now turning its attention to the question of day schools or training homes where girls from the elementary schools can obtain practical training in the care and management of babies and young children. A scheme has been drawn up which recommends a year's course at a Domestic Economy School, to be followed by from 6 to 12 months at a well conducted crèche or similar institution having already the charge of babies. It is hoped that this scheme will shortly be put into practice in an experimental way, and that either the L.C.C. or other local authorities may take up the idea and work it out on the same lines as the day trade schools for girls already mentioned.

The Committee has also published a series of 1d. pamphlets on the Labour Laws for Women in various countries. Other pamphlets on subjects of industrial interest are published from time to time as the necessity arises. It also publishes every year a list of members and friends who have offered to give lectures and start debates on industrial subjects. A small postage fee is charged for arranging these lectures, and societies having funds are encouraged to give a donation to the Council. The audiences vary greatly from guilds of women co-operators and girls' clubs to debating societies and drawing-room meetings. This part of the work is educational in the strict sense.

Chairman – Mrs. J. Ramsay Macdonald.
Hon. Sec. – Miss E. M. Zimmern.

THE LEGAL COMMITTEE

The Legal Committee has two main duties: to promote legislation and watch administration in the interests of the working women and girls. Its practical action takes the form of getting questions put in the House of Parliament, amendments to Bills promoted, petitions and deputations received and public attention called to matters of urgent reform in the press and elsewhere. It drafted the Home Work Regulation Bill, which was introduced by Colonel Denny, and is now in the charge of Mr. J. Ramsay Macdonald in Parliament. This measure advocates the licensing of all home workers, by which means the inspection and enforcement of sanitary conditions in their homes would be better secured than is at present the case, and the casual worker, who does so much to depress the conditions, would be discouraged. The Committee publishes leaflets explaining the needs of women, and what local authorities can do for them, which have been sent to all candidates before Borough and County Council elections. The Committee also reports breaches of the Factory and Workshop Act, in co-operation with the Investigation Committee, to the Home Office. It also considers the Report of the Hon. Solicitor on cases referred to him and decides what further steps may be taken.

Chairman – G. C. Cope, Barrister-at-Law.
Hon. Sec. – Mrs. J. Ramsay Macdonald.

Organisations

THE GIRLS' CLUB LIBRARY

In earlier days the Council founded some organisations for practical work, the Clubs Industrial Association, the Physical Drill for Working Girls, the Girls' Club Library, the Picture Lending Library, and the A.T.C., an association of trained domestic workers. Meanwhile conditions were altered by the formation of many new societies, and the Physical Drill organisation, after 13 years' close connection with the Council, now has a separate life of its own under Miss Clara James (21, Rochester Square, N.W.), while the demand for the Picture Lending Library was found to exist only in theory. The Girls' Club Library – a loan collection of books constantly renewed and brought up to date – distributes boxes of books twice a year to any club paying a small fee. The selection of books is made by the clubs themselves.

Hon. Librarian – Miss L. A. Black, 7, John Street.

THE CLUBS INDUSTRIAL ASSOCIATION

The Clubs Industrial Association numbers 45 clubs, and exists to promote the principle that the industrial life of working girls can be affected by the educational work done in clubs. For this purpose club leaders and girls are helped to acquire knowledge of the Factory Law by means of lectures, leaflets, &c., and the establishment of citizenship classes, and committees are formed with a view to carry out investigation work. The 45 clubs which are affiliated undertake to report infringements of industrial law when they come under their notice. Three Social Meetings a year are also held.

President – Mrs. Amie Hicks   *Vice-President* – Miss Chambers
Hon. Sec – Hon. Lily Montagu

THE A.T.C. AND DOMESTIC WORKERS' ASSOCIATION

The A.T.C. and Domestic workers' Registered Employment Agency, London County Council, is an association of domestic workers of 25 different classes now numbering some 600 women. Founded originally to help a few char-women – one of the most helpless classes of the community – to get and keep work by doing it better, it has developed in response to a growing demand on the part of employers, while at the same time giving valuable assistance to the Central Unemployed Body and the Distress Committees of London.

The A.T.C. has a separate Report and Balance Sheet and its own Advisory Committee.

Chairman – Mrs. Frederic Franklin
Hon. Sec. – Miss F. Potter, 7, John Street, Tel. 1151 City

Applications for Membership, offers of help in some branch of the work, as well as Subscriptions and Donations, however small in amount, will be gratefully acknowledged by the Secretary.

Cheques and Post-Office Orders should be crossed "London and Westminster Bank, Temple Bar Branch."

Investigations

The results of the Council's investigations were often written up in articles by Council members and appeared in the *Women's Industrial News* as well as other periodicals. The following is an article on laundry work written by Margaret MacDonald. It appeared in the June 1907 *WIN** and is an example of the type of inquiry undertaken by the WIC. It also shows the immense amount of information collected by the Council's investigators during their inquiries on the working conditions for women in London trades. The article is followed by a short list, appearing in the same issue of *WIN*, of the trades investigated or being investigated by the Council and thus shows the scope of its inquiries.

REPORT ON ENQUIRY INTO CONDITIONS OF WORK IN LAUNDRIES

This enquiry has extended over more than a year, and the report was not published sooner because the investigators felt for some time that whilst they had visited a representative number of laundries they had not met enough of the workers to get their side of the question adequately stated. As the result, however, of paying special attention to this difficulty we have now a somewhat better proportion of workers amongst our reports, and have also seen Bible women, leaders of clubs, and others who come a great deal in contact with women and girls from laundries. The laundries visited by our

* *WIN*, **39** (1907), pp. 629–43.

investigators total nearly 150, and about many of these we have very full information.

The laundry trade is in an interesting transition stage. Having been a small hand industry, it is gradually becoming as much a factory trade as any which is worked by power machinery. I have just visited the Laundry Exhibition at the Agricultural Hall, where machinery is shown which will do every part of the washing and drying, and where the latest pronouncement of engineers and chemists on the science of the laundry is shown. Well-to-do gentlemen in top hats were walking about with knowing criticisms of this, that and the other device, but there were also a good many poorly dressed people looking at the exhibits. The aspect of one shabby care-worn widow struck my fancy. She looked anxious and frightened as she hastily slipped past the great array of whirling cylinders and rolling bands. I pictured her to myself as the owner of a small hand laundry in some poor street, who had come along in an energetic moment to try and get some hints for her trade, but who was overpowered by the modern up-to-date methods in evidence in the galleries. She would think of her own rough appliances and her own unremitting labour as she looked at the electrical drying machine whose "capacity when dealing with shirts is from 650 to 850 per hour, according to the temperature used, and it is only necessary to have one or two attendants to feed in the articles to be dried and remove those which are dried"; or at the collar steamer and press (steam heated), whose output "is at least 600 collars per hour." She would shrink into herself as she remembered that she had dared to hope for help from the exhibits; and would feel that instead of friendly counsel she had found a giant which was destined to swallow her up and those like her, and against whose relentless competition she would be powerless to strive much longer. As a matter of fact one of our investigators found a family who kept a small hand laundry so excited about the competition at the big laundries that father, mother and daughter all talked at once about the iniquities of the new system, and the visitor could get no coherent answers to her questions. Quoth Mrs. X, "Put a girl in the laundry trade! Might as well put her in the workhouse at once, I wouldn't put a cat in it! It's them steam laundries have all the trade and they do their work by machinery and children. . . . I have been in this business 20 years; it was a good thing when I started. Now I wish I hadn't put my daughter to it. . . . There ought to be a law to forbid these laundries."

Yet though the march of machinery and science goes on altering the trade, without any law to stop it, the process is gradual, and our investigators found every kind and size of laundry, from the living room where a single woman was working, through all varieties of hand laundry, steam laundry, and mixed hand and machine laundry, to the huge establishments with two or three hundred employees – one, for instance, having 250 women and 70 men working for it; another 250 women and only 6 men.

After all, the machinery is never likely to have it all its own way, for the most careful and artistic work must always be done by hand. As one successful employer said, "People will pay if their clothes are well ironed and delicate things are not spoiled. The trade to seek is the most delicate and difficult; that is where the profits come in, and people pay 1/- and 1/6 to have silk and lace nightdresses properly washed and ironed. But it needs great skill. You really want a girl who enjoys delicate work. Most things can be done by machine; but some handwashing is needed; shirts and all delicate things and 'finery' are better done by hand. The best work and the best profits are to those who have learnt how to combine machine and hand work." The ideal here sketched is not often reached, but even in ordinary plain work the hand laundry has not yet been driven from the field; whilst machines can of course never be taught to do the packing and sorting of goods. One manageress in a laundry employing 30 women told us that her employer had no calender machine in the place at present. He was thinking of putting one in but was afraid of losing his high-class custom if he did, for the west-end society people liked to know that all their tablecloths, etc., were ironed by hand, and "certainly it is much better for the tablecloths."

The geographical distribution of our laundries is interesting. In the centre of London you may search for a laundry as for a needle in a hay stack. We did discover one or two even within the City itself, but mostly it was suburban journeys that our investigators had to take. A day in Peckham or Hampstead, in Battersea or Wood Green would bring in a sheaf of reports. Even North Kensington which used to be a famous laundry centre is almost too central now, and the work is gradually going further west to Acton, where whole streets seem almost filled with laundries. It is not only London customers who deal with London. Much washing comes in from country houses and provincial districts, and the seasonal nature of the custom of wealthy clients is partly obviated by the fact that so many send their clothes still to the

London laundry when they themselves are out of town. On the other hand only two employers mentioned that laundry work is sometimes sent abroad, both of them giving Paris as its destination. Nor did we find any trace of the pig-tailed Chinese, whom anyone who knows our colonies associates so naturally with the washing of dirty linen.

The main lines of our inquiry tended towards two practical objects. We wanted first to find out what openings there are for skilled workers and for the training of such workers; and secondly we wanted to be able to promote and to criticise proposals for further legal regulation of laundries with information based on first-hand knowledge of present conditions.

To understand the kind of opening for girls in the trade we must know the different divisions of the work. First, when the goods are brought in by collecting vans, or, in a poor street, perhaps by the customers themselves, they have to be checked to see that they are correctly entered, to mark any tears or blemishes which might be afterwards blamed to the Laundry if not noted at first; then they are sorted according to colour and texture. This is often an unpleasant work, as the clothes are soiled, but it is also quite skilled work; for upon it depends not only the accurate book-keeping of the business, but also the proper treatment of woollen, as contrasted with cotton goods, of children's muslin pinafores, as against sheets and counterpanes, and so on. The sorters usually do the packing also, and a quick memory and neat fingers are needed in order that every one may have their own clothes returned, and may receive them in good condition. The actual washers come next. Where there are heavy washing machines men are employed. Sometimes the washing and rinsing is entirely in their hands; sometimes women assist them in the lighter parts. It is recorded that old women are employed to wash the flannels in some places, whilst in others the young girls are set to "dabble" for an hour or two in the washing room to initiate them gently into its mysteries. In hand laundries the work is done throughout by women.

Next comes the wringing, whether it is done by hand or machine. Some of the machines for getting the wet out of the clothes are just like those one sees in a sugar mill turning the sweet syrup into crystals, the force upon which both depend being centrifugal. The humble mangle has developed into the calender, which is fed with damp clothes from a sort of trough, and rolls them out smooth and shining. A visit to a well-appointed laundry, or to the Laundry Exhibition, gives one visions of the time when we shall put our soiled clothes in at one end of a machine and they will come out at the other end spotless and fresh, and folded, just as the famous pig who goes in alive at one end and comes out as tasty sausages at the other. There are all sorts of contrivances for drying, from the line in the backyard to the endless chain which passes through a hot chamber. Some of the work in putting things in heated drying rooms is very trying, but the latest inventions obviate altogether the need for the workers to come in contact with the great heat themselves, whilst generally more consideration is shown than formerly, we were told by an experienced manageress, in forbidding workers to go into the drying chambers at all, even for a minute, when they are fully heated.

Ironing is another chief division of the industry. Here, too, we have every stage from hand work to the ironing machine, the principal intermediate step being where the irons are guided by hand, but are heated and worked by machinery. Then we come back to the packers, and the week's work is done. Some laundries give out part of their work to be done elsewhere, and we found some small laundries which practically existed on this overflow from large establishments.

We have particulars from 96 laundries about the training of girls. Of these, 55 told us that they do not take learners at all, some because they have not room, some because they have not time, two because "it doesn't pay to take them," and the remainder without any reason given. Of the 41 who do take young girls as learners, no general statement as to conditions can be made. Some gave elaborate scales of wages paid as the girl grew older. In one large firm they take apprentices for every branch of work, each girl being taught one branch in nine months; for the first three months she receives one-third of the ordinary rate of pay; for the second three months, two-thirds of the ordinary rate; and for the third three months, three-quarters of the ordinary rate. Only nine firms say that they ask a premium with their apprentices, three asking a guinea, one half a guinea, one fifteen shillings, one eleven shillings, one ten shillings, another ten shillings deposit, which is returned at the end of three months if the work is satisfactory, whilst the ninth asks two guineas for teaching the whole trade, and half a guinea for teaching one special branch. There is a tenth firm which demands the modest sum of two shillings and sixpence, but this can hardly be dignified by the name of a premium. In this case, and in a good many of those which ask no premium at all, girls have to serve a month or more for nothing. A good many, however, get as much as two shillings and sixpence or four shillings a week from the very first. In one place, where the premium is one guinea, this is given back if the girl does not suit, whereas, if she stays, she is trained for three months, and during that time gets what she earns on Mondays and Saturdays for pocket-money. A large laundry in South London takes on apprentices only in the slack season, when there is time to teach. The packers and sorters in this firm pay no premium but give two months work free, and then start at five shillings a week; while the colar and shirt ironers pay one guinea premium, give two months free, and then are put on piece-work.

Our Council is specially interested in the possibilities of teaching trades to girls in technical schools, and as it had been suggested that laundry work, as a trade, might usefully be taught by the London County Council, the opinion of employers and workers was asked on this point. Forty-six were in favour of classes; thirty-four expressed an opinion against them. The statistics as to their answers are, however, of little value, as most of them had evidently not thought of the matter at all before, and gave answers more or less at random. One employee who was interviewed began by being decidedly in favour of classes, but when two of her friends came in and threw cold water on the suggestion she changed at once and thought it would be of no use at all. Many of the employers and managers were almost equally uncertain. Two opposed the idea because they seemed to scent competition by the schools catering for custom. A great many were in favour just because, as they said, they would be glad to know where to apply for skilled workers, others because they thought the classes might train forewomen and manageresses for them. Some were prejudiced against classes because of their contempt for the present laundry teaching in the day schools or polytechnics, but their objections were modified when it was explained that the present classes are not supposed to teach girls for the trade, but for their own domestic washing, and that in a trade school teachers with experience of trade methods would be employed. Only one objected to classes on the ground that it would "send up the rates," but a good many expressed the fear that it would be useless to establish them because the girls would not go. Others again maintained that the work could only be taught in a business laundry, whilst four said that it would be more practicable to give apprenticeships to girls in good laundries than to establish classes outside for them. A select number of the employers were really interested in the question, and gave valuable hints and advice and promises of help in the management and planning of such classes.

A practical result has already come from this part of the enquiry. A special class has just been started at the Borough Polytechnic for the employees of one of the employers visited by Mrs. Oakeshott. This employer is very much impressed with the need for superior knowledge amongst laundry workers. He wants them to know more about manipulation of the machinery so that they can themselves prevent mistakes or correct faults in its working. He wants them also to know thoroughly how to treat the different materials and textures of different garments, and he wants them to know something of the chemistry of the various ingredients which are used for washing, bleaching, starching, &c. He is putting every facility in the way of his employees to attend the classes planned for them. It is also arranged that the work shall be carried on in consultation with the science teacher, so that theory and practice may help each other. For the new Day Trade School centre which will shortly be established for girls by the London County Council, laundry work is one of the industries chosen, and the experiment will thus, we hope, shortly be actually at work, with an expert teacher, and advice from scientific men on one side, and business experience. A smaller experiment on these lines is already in working order at the Wandsworth Common Deaf and Dumb Residential School, where some of the scholars are being prepared successfully to earn a livelihood by laundry work. The laundry in this school is a hand laundry, with some revolving machines which are not driven by power, and the learners are girls from 13 to 16 years old.

When we are contemplating starting girls in life in the laundry trade, or supporting schools to enable them to enter it, we naturally feel a responsibility as regards the chances of advancement to those who take up the work, and also the class of workers whom they will have as companions.

Under the heading of prospects, our investigators usually report that there are good openings for manageresses or forewomen and that it is difficult to fill these positions. The pay recorded as given for these more responsible positions is from £1 upwards. The mother of two superintendents who was interviewed said that one of her daughters was getting £2 and the other 38/-, but that a head manageress can earn quite £5. Both her daughters are engaged to be married, but neither intends to be married till the young men are in good positions. The mother said that girls who become heads of departments begin in the office and never work with other employees. On this point we have a good deal of conflicting evidence. One employer told us that forewomen practically never rose from amongst the hands; the latter might be able to supervise all right but would never have the necessary command. Forewomen, he added, generally have been through a three or six months' course at a laundry and often have been teachers and nurses before. On the other hand, in two cases, the manageress of fair-sized laundries had risen from the ranks themselves. One of these told me that her parents had paid £5 for her to learn the trade right through; she began as an ordinary worker but had shown special aptitude and risen to a responsible post. She spoke with quite professional enthusiasm of the various parts of her craft. At many places we were told that a capable girl could easily rise to be forewoman. There was often, but not always, the qualification that she must be in the packing and sorting department to get this chance. Another kind of promotion which was reported to us several times was from the sorting and packing room to one of the receiving offices of a big laundry. This is quite a separate part of the business and the workers in it come under the Shop Hours Act, not the Factory Act. Of course there is also the possibility that if a girl learns all the branches of her trade well she may start a small laundry of her own.

With regard to the wages of employees we were given a great deal of detailed information, but unfortunately we have no full records taken from wages books.

In the great majority of cases the wages are paid according to piece rates, a few by time, and some firms have both time and piece rates.

For sorters and packers the highest limit given is 25s. a week, and this is given in a fairly large proportion of cases. The lowest recorded is 4s., but this was for young girls; in the same laundry, however, 11s. was given as the highest pay for this class of work. On the average, the full week's wages seem to range anywhere between 10s and 20s. for sorters and packers. We have very few estimates of weekly wages for washers; those we have only range from 7s. to 9s., but their daily wage is quoted variously as 2s. 3d., 2s. 6d., 2s. 9d. and 3s. – 2s. 6d. being the most usual. One employer estimated that washers get 1s. or 2s. less each week than ironers. With regard to calender hands we have even less detailed information, but what we have gives a wider range – 7s., 8s., 9s. a week up to 15s. or 17s.; whilst one manager at a firm where 160 girls are employed reported that the calender hands get 1¼d. an hour to begin with, rising to 3d. an hour, making 18s. a week. The same manager stated that ironers began at 4s., and that every ironer could rise to 30s. weekly, but that most girls were content with 16s., and did not attempt to earn more. In a good many cases the weekly rates of ironers were given us as running over £1. Their daily wages are variously recorded as 2s. 3d., 2s. 6d., 3s., 3s. 6d., 4s., 4s. 6d., 5s., and 6s. a day; the latter figures are, however, explained as earned only by the best and quickest workers. We have a good many details of piece rates for collars, shirts, etc., but these of course are valueless unless one has also the details of the machines used, if machine labour, as the rates for this vary according to the capacity of the machine.

It must be remembered in reading these wages that the daily rates are hardly ever paid for the full 5½ days a week, often for only 3 or 4 days, whilst a great many laundries suffer from slack time in winter. Overtime is often paid by an extra 3d. an hour.

One elderly woman, an ironer on piecework, seen early in November, showed us the little paper bags in which she had received her money each week for the past six weeks. She had to ask for 1s. or 1s. 6d. in advance each week, owing to being very poor. Two pence were deducted each week for the use of the dining-room in the laundry though she does not dine there. Her weekly average for these six weeks had been 6s. 3¾d.

Much of the work is paid daily, but a nurse who has been in charge for more than twenty years at a crèche where the babies are almost all the children of laundry women, finds that weekly payment is getting more common and that the mothers now often ask her to wait till the end of the week for her money as they are not paid till then.

As to the class of workers with whom a laundry girl has to associate it is impossible to give any sweeping generalisation. The workers we have seen vary from some of the roughest and most ignorant to some of the most refined and intelligent girls whom one could find anywhere in London. Reading one report one is tempted to say that the small laundry hands are rougher than those in steam laundries, but then one comes upon a descrip-tion of a superior well-managed hand laundry as compared with a set of girls and women from a factory laundry who are rough and careless in their manners. One might have thought that having to deal with so much dirty linen would tend to repel superior girls, yet it is just in the sorting room that a better class of girls is found in almost every laundry. The real solution of the problem is that it depends more upon the employer what sort of workers he or she gets, than upon the nature of the employment, and in placing girls from a trade school one would naturally try to recommend them to firms which are well managed.

Beer drinking is one of the things which has given laundry work a bad name, but the custom of giving beer money or allowing beer to be fetched in during working hours is rather dying out. The work is specially calculated to make the workers thirsty, but many employers now supply mineral waters or oatmeal water rather than beer. In one laundry I remember seeing the beer cans and the teapots reposing amicably side by side on a shelf above the ironing boards, but in quite a number of cases we were told that beer inside had been forbidden. "Subbing" is another custom, not altogether unconnected with beer drinking, which used to be more prevalent in the trade than it is now. "Subbing" means the payment of part wages before they are due at the end of the week, some of the women do not resist the temptation to ask for subs that they may spend on drink, others no doubt find them handy for more necessary purposes. It is especially the married women who want subs. The custom is very unsatisfactory both to the employer and to the worker who gets 2/- or 3/- less at the end of the week than her full pay. Some of the employers organised in a Laundry Association tried unsuccessfully to combine to put it down; we are told that when they held a meeting for the purpose they had to be guarded by a strong force of police, so unpopular was the suggestion. But others have stopped it without such difficulty, whilst some only allow it on Wednesdays or some other specified day. One employer met the difficulty by getting the women each to subscribe 1/- a week and thus raising £1 a week, which was lent to each woman in turn to set her straight for the current week so that she was able to overtake her arrears, and wait for her money at the end of the week from that time forward.

The greater number of the workers in the trade are married. The census figures, 1901, show for London 20,158 unmarried workers, 27,204 married. Some employers report that they prefer girls, others that they like women to come back after they are married as they get experienced workers in that way. One says that he employs two married women (out of 32 employees) but would not have them from choice as "the baby is always the excuse if they come late or stop away altogether." Some report that the trade is a convenient one for married women as they only work three or four days a week, the ironers, for instance, often come in early on Tuesday or even Wednesday, whilst the packers and sorters may have short time in the middle of the week.

We had a good deal said to us about the evil effect on the men of having their wives in laundries, for they leave their wives to be the wage earners as well as the housewives of the family. No doubt the lazy habits sometimes begin during a period of genuine unemployment, when the man gradually loses his self respect and drifts down into being a loafer, and continues to live upon the self-sacrificing industry of the wife. But whether the husband is morally to blame or not, the effect upon the wife of her double share of duty in the laundry and at home is most disastrous. Especially is this the case where there are young children. We have had heartrending tales told to us of the mothers who actually have worked up to within a few minutes of their confinement – worked at wringing machines into which they have to lift piles of heavy wet clothes, or standing long hours at the ironing tables. One manageress told us how the women tried to hide their condition from her for fear she should forbid them to come, since they saw starvation for themselves and the elder children as the only alternative to the heavy strain of work. After the birth of the baby the mother hurries back again to work, some-times, there seems no doubt, before the legal period of four weeks is over, though the law has on the whole a good moral effect in keeping this four weeks free. More than one employer or manageress was very strongly in favour of limiting the time *before* childbirth during which the mother may be employed, and extending it for a longer period afterwards. With the long hours of laundry work it is almost incredible that a woman just before or after her confinement can also do her housework without serious injury to her health, and the actual cases cited to us showed that often the results are very serious.

Our question regarding the general healthiness of the trade was usually answered differently according to whether the person asked was an employer or a worker. The employers mostly say that the work is healthy, and that the girls get used to the long hours of standing. Some of them, and of their managers, acknowledge, however, that it needs a strong constitution. Some of the workers owned to excellent health; but several of them told a very different tale. Rheumatism and bronchial complaints are the special illnesses mentioned. One elderly woman crippled with rheumatism herself strongly advised young girls not to go into the trade. She ascribed her own ill health to it, and said that the ill effects of laundry work are felt more afterwards than at the time. "Though we had boards to stand on, we could not keep our legs dry; sometimes we were wet up to the shoulders with steam." This referred however, to hand laundry work. Another, a woman of 30, was suffering from rheumatoid affection of the joints, her hands being swollen and helpless. She had worked four years in a machine laundry and was all right there, but had then gone into a small laundry full of steam and this had ruined her health. Another worker again was found to be suffering from rheumatism and said that the work was a great strain on the muscles of the back and shoulders. The crèche nurse already mentioned, says that inspection has improved the sanitary condition of the laundries, and she hears much less than she used to of women standing ankle-deep in water all day. Our investigators report unfavourably on some of the laundries visited as being very damp and steaming. The simple truth is probably expressed by the manager who declares the work to be "healthy, if the laundry is well managed." There is no question, however, that the work is heavy and laborious.

This brings us on to the question of hours, and here we gathered evidence of most varied customs. Our readers are probably aware that the existing law allows these varieties, the daily limit of hours for women over 18 years old being 14 hours, including meal times, with 2 hours extra on 30 days in the year, so that on one in every twelve days the law allows 14 hours actual work, exclusive of meal times. The weekly limit is 60 hours a week, in addition to such overtime as is allowed, which must not exceed 6 hours in any one week. The elasticity allowed makes it almost impossible for the inspectors to enforce even this very meagre regulation of hours, for if they find the workers late at night one day in the week it is very difficult to prove that they have not made up for this by short time earlier in the week, unless the workers are willing to give evidence; whilst their fear of dismissal makes it difficult to get them to be witnesses in court.

As I have shown already, different classes of workers are busiest or most slack on different days in the week, since sorting must precede washing and ironing. In some cases, however, this difficulty is met by arranging the customers in different shifts, some sending their clothes on Monday, some later in the week. It is hardly worth while to give a statistical table of the hours reported to us, as unless they could be more fully checked than we have any means of doing those given by the employers or managers — these, as I have said, being the majority of our informants — would probably err on the side of shortness. But we are glad to note that apart from statistical exactitude there does seem real improvement in the regularity and shortness of the day's work. Many of the laundries work no more than the regular factory hours, some say they never work as much, and this gives us reason to hope that the Government proposals for further legal regulation of laundries . . ., will easily bring into line places which at present sadly need shorter hours. Such a place is the firm whose forewoman told us they never worked later than 9 p.m., but who afterwards said that three hands slept in as they might be wanted at any time to carry out telegraphic orders in the middle of the night from hotels, &c. This same forewoman thought the trade a "noble" but much maligned one. She expressed special concern about the moral behaviour of the girls, who were really a specially respectable looking set of workers. She "tried to make them thoughtful for others," and had various missionary boxes; she had talked to them about these and tried to make them give 1d. weekly but they rather rebelled; she then made them give ½d., and they have done so ever since. She is reported as "evidently quite a motherly but rather a managing woman." I do not know how she reconciles her missionary conscience with keeping girls working illegally at night. Another manageress left one place because she was made to keep girls so late at night. She complains that the inspectors do not pay nearly enough visits to the laundries; but acknowledges that in any case it is difficult for them to check employers who deliberately deceive them by keeping the laundry all dark and closed in front whilst the workers are working at the back. Several other employers or forewomen confessed to breaking the law. One magnanimously explained that she rarely did so, and that she has forbidden her forewoman to do so "except under extreme circumstances." Another who acknowledged cheating the factory inspector by locking the gate and keeping the workers till midnight, said, "What are you to do? If I hadn't got the work home that week, there would have been no work next week for them to do." These long and late hours, whether within or without the legal limit, are frightfully exhausting for the workers. A deaf and dumb girl whom I know was kept on Saturday till midnight, and her mother and sister who anxiously went to seek her were not allowed to fetch her away until she actually fainted at her work and had to be taken home.

For late Saturday work some of the poorer customers are responsible. They bring the husband's shirt front in at the last minute and want it ready for Sunday. Some of the laundries in self defence put a notice outside "No work given out on Sundays." If they had the support of the law, by the inclusion in the Government Bill of our proposal that 4 p.m. should be the extreme limit on Saturday, they would all be able to insist upon more consideration from the customers. It is, however, by no means the poor customers who are the most inconsiderate. At one firm, for instance, we found that a noble Lord, a prominent member of the House of Peers, had just sent in 500 serviettes on Monday afternoon to be returned on Tuesday evening. We had other complaints from laundries with first-class custom, of work being sent one day and a telegram following to say it must be returned next day. When several customers do this sort of thing at once, the Factory Act is broken. Hotels and clubs are worse still, for they always want their sheets or collars and shirts back the next day.

We had some complaints of the long and irregular hours worked in the small laundries which are at present exempt from legal regulation if not more than two workers who are not members of the family are employed. Some of these complaints were from the point of view of the hardship entailed upon their employee; others were made from larger laundries which object to their competition. Still stronger objection was made in several cases to the competition of charity laundries, which are partly subsidised by charity, and which at present are outside the law.

We met with considerable difference of opinion when we touched upon the delicate ground of further legal regulations. Some employers and managers pooh-poohed the idea that the present hours could hurt anybody in ordinary health – "the women are wonderfully strong." Others expressed the opinion, some of them rather fearfully and confidentially, that the hours allowed are too long. However, as I have already indicated, we have a considerable weight of evidence that the application of legal regulations to laundries, which dates from 1891, has improved the sanitary conditions, lengthened the time during which the mothers stay away after child-birth, and shortened the hours of work or at any rate caused them to be distributed better over the week.

I think one may sum up the material results of the investigation as proving:–

(*a*) That there is an opening for improvement in the training of girls for the work, and that it is worth while to try and meet this by the establishment of trade day schools.

(*b*) That the present legislative protection, whilst it has done considerable good, is open to great improvement, both by making the provisions of the law less elastic, and by increasing the staff of inspectors who administer it.

Margaret E. MacDonald.

REPORTS ON TRADES

Reports of women's work in the following trades have appeared in back numbers of the *Women's Industrial News*. Except Nos. 8, 13 and 18, the enquiries were the work of the Investigation Committee of the Women's Industrial Council. Price 4½d. each post free. Those marked * are o. p.

1. Fur-pulling (*News*, March 1898; *Nineteenth Century*, November 1897).
2. Typing (*News*, June 1898 and September 1898).
3. Boot Trade (*News*, September 1898).
4. Printing Trades (*News*, Dec. 1898 and Dec. 1904; *Economic Journal*, June 1899).
5. Straw Plait Industry (*News*, Sept. 1899).
6. What Occupations are taken up by Girls on Leaving School? (*News*, March 1900).
7. *Upholstery (*News*, March 1900; *Open Doors for Women Workers*, 1903).
8. Birmingham Pen Trade (*News*, June 1900).
9. Women's Work in Dustyards (*Economic Journal*, Sept. 1900).
10. *Cigar-making (*News*, Sept. 1900 and Dec. 1900; *Economic Journal*, Dec. 1900).
11. *Domestic Service (*News*, March 1900, June 1901; *Nineteenth Century*, June, 1903).
12. Pharmacy (*News*, June 1901).
13. The Clothing Trade in Amsterdam (*News*, Sept. 1901, Dec. 1901).
14. French Polishing (*News*, March 1902).
15. Sanitary Inspecting (*News*, March 1902).
16. Machining (*News*, March 1903).

17. Artificial Flower-making (*News*, June 1903; *Economic Journal*, March 1903).
18. Fruit-picking (*News*, Sept. 1903).
19. Jewel Case Making (*News*, June 1904).
20. Embroidery, Part I. (*News*, Sept. 1904).
21. Tailoring (*News*, Sept. and Dec. 1905; *Economic Journal*, 1904).
22. Millinery (*News*, March 1906).
23. Jewellery (*News*, March 1907).
24. Laundry Work (*News*, June 1907).

The Committee have also partially investigated the following trades, and the information collected may be consulted in manuscript at the office, after written application to the Secretary.

1. Lacquering.	8.	Confectionery.
2. Box-making.	9.	Haircutting.
3. Military Cap Making.	10.	Boot-making.
4. Dress-making.	11.	Jewel Case Lining.
5. Mantle-making.	12.	Electrical Fittings Making.
6. Military Tailoring.	13.	Gentlemen's Hat Lining.
7. Leather Working.	14.	Laundry Work and Ironing.

A Review of the Report of the Technical Education Board for 1903 of the Women's Industrial Council

As the result of these inquiries, the Council often had recommendations to make to government bodies concerning industrial and educational matters relating to women workers. The following excerpt from the March 1904 *WIN*★ written by Grace Oakeshott, Secretary of the Council's Technical Training Committee, is part of a larger review of the work of the London Technical Education Board for 1903. It contains some of the Council's views on technical education for girls.

✳

★ *WIN*, 26 (March 1904), pp. 413–15.

AT the formation of the Technical Training Committee in 1900, two distinct lines of work were laid down:—

1. To discover the nature of the technical training given to girls of the industrial class at Technical Institutes.

2. To discover the skilled trades for women, in which technical training would be an advantage.

It was no small task that the Technical Training Committee had therefore undertaken; and it is one which it has by no means completed. It entailed visits to the leading Technical Institutes, and as far as might be, enquiry into the existing classes, their *raison d'etre*, their success and results. The work, however, which was more difficult and lengthier, was the enquiry into skilled trades and the advantage of technical training in any given trade. This involved an enquiry into every skilled trade open to women in London, and as they are numerous, it is still incomplete. Thanks, however, to the past work of the Investigation Committee, and to its steady continuance of investigation, it is slowly being accomplished.

The Technical Training Committee, therefore, seeks to be the medium for expressing the educational, though the unrealised and unexpressed, needs of the industrial worker to the authority that supplies these needs. They have by means of their enquiries into skilled trades, their interviews with employers, their connection with Factory Club leaders, with the girls themselves, with the Voluntary Employment Agencies seeking to place girls in desirable employments, a means of getting a very accurate picture of what is needed and the way the need can be met. Their interim letters of July, 1902, to the Technical Education Board, and their report to the Women's Industrial Council, printed in the *Women's Industrial News* in December, 1902, expressed to some extent their views as to the possible improvements and developments of existing technical training.

To the principles and suggestions laid down in that letter and report, the Technical Training Committee still adhere, though their information is amplified.

The articles which appeared in the *Daily Chronicle* in January and February 1903, afterwards reprinted as a supplement to the *Women's Industrial News*, gave further expression to these views, and gave illustrations of the technical training for girls abroad, and how favourably it compared with ours.

The Advisory Sub-Committee appointed by the Technical Education

Board to enquire into the technical instruction for women issued a series of questions in the spring of this year to various individuals interested in this subject. It may be well here to recapitulate as briefly as possible the recommendation made by the Technical Training Committee to the Technical Education Board, both in answer to these questions and in various letters.

Before making any recommendations, however, the Technical Training Committee called the attention of the Technical Training Board to what may be termed the industrial attitude of women:— "namely, the lack of that ambition which should make them eager for thorough training, the tendency to undersell men and the willingness to perform the unskilled branches of a trade, resulting from the impression that they will remain in industry for so short a time." Further, that the long hours worked by girls in workrooms or factories frequently make attendance at evening classes impossible and even undesirable; girls naturally prefer classes of a recreative nature.

With these facts in mind the Technical Training Committee made the following recommendations:—

WITH REGARD TO INDUSTRIAL TRAINING:—

1. That for the reasons given above, Trade Evening Classes will never be very successful, but industrial training might be of great value if girls passed direct from elementary schools to day technical schools.

These might be of two kinds:—

(a) Day technical schools on the lines of the Shoreditch Boys' Technical Day School, where instruction is given with a special view to future industrial life, combined with general education.

(b) Half-time day classes, enabling girls to be employed in the morning, while learning a trade and continuing their general education in the afternoon and evening.

2. That to reach the child of poor parents, education must be free, and in necessitous cases, maintenance grants must be given.

3. That until the disabilities for teaching trades be removed, not much can be done.

WITH REGARD TO DOMESTIC ECONOMY CENTRES:—

1. Domestic Economy Evening and Afternoon Classes:—

(*a*) That instruction in the care and management of infants and young children be given.

(*b*) That the Board extend its teaching at girls' clubs, settlements and mothers' meetings.

2. Domestic Economy Day Schools:–

(*a*) That teaching in the care and management of infants and young children be given.

(*b*) That the curriculum in these schools is too specialised and not sufficiently educational.

(i.) That too much time is spent at laundry (viz., 6 hours a week).

(ii.) That more time be given to physical exercises (1 hour a week when possible is given now).

(iii.) That drawing to scale and measure be introduced.

(iv.) That some subject of interest – viz., citizenship classes – be taught.

3. That day schools on the lines of the Domestic Economy Schools for training girls in the care and management of infants and young children be established.

4. That training for Day Domestic Helpers be given.

WITH REGARD TO THE ADVERTISEMENT OF THESE CLASSES:–

1. That the Board should come more closely into touch with Elementary Schools, namely,

(*a*) That lists of skilled trades be hung in the elementary schools with the technical institute where training could be obtained.

(*b*) That the co-operation of managers, head-mistresses and parents be sought in encouraging girls to continue their education and to train.

(*c*) That girls and their parents be addressed on the subject.

2. That employers be circularised about the classes in existence and be asked to allow their employees to leave in time to enable them to attend these classes.

Lastly the Technical Training Committee recommended the Board to consider the desirability of women playing a greater part in the technical instruction of this country; and suggested that more than one lady member should be coopted on to the Technical Education Board; and that women should be appointed as Superintendents of Polytechnics on an equal footing with men. . . .

The Councils inquiries into the conditions of homeworkers

The Council undertook two investigations into the conditions of homework, one published in 1897 and the second in 1908. A summary of the results of the first inquiry where more than 400 cases were visited, was given in *The Contemporary Review* in December 1897.* As the article concluded, the aim was 'to set forth afresh, in some detail, the plain facts of the destitute life about us which we well know but fail to realise'. Subsequently, the Council drew up a Home Work Bill which was introduced in Parliament, for the first time in 1899. The second selection, published in 1902, provides the reader with the Council's stand on the issue. In 1914, L. Wyatt-Papworth, the Council's General Secretary, claimed that this bill helped 'to prepare the way for the public interest culminating in the Trade Boards Act of 1909'.

✳

Women's Home Industries

Most of our discussions and disputes on the labour question relate to the aristocracy of labour – to those who are readily organised into powerful trade-unions, and can resist, wisely or otherwise, reduction of wages, fight for shorter hours, and carry on regular campaigns against their employers, sometimes even against their more powerful adversaries – machinery and foreign competition. These great controversies of the industrial world touch only the upper ranks of toilers. Even the historical strikes of unskilled labourers, of dockers and seamen, difficult as they are to conduct, leave unstirred the lower depths of daily work; rank behind rank stand masses of helpless women, generally too poor and ignorant to organise, to struggle, or even to remonstrate, mere slaves to the imperious necessity of starvation wages.

It is never, therefore, out of place to call attention again to this poorest stratum of the population, jammed between famine and the workhouse. A new inquiry, conducted on the most modern principle of actual detailed

---

* See *The Contemporary Review*, LXXII (December 1897), pp. 880–6 and The Women's Industrial Council, *How to Deal with Home Work*, 4 pp.

examination, has recently been made by the Women's Industrial Council, into the condition of about four hundred London women who earn money by working at home, and it is proposed in a few pages to summarise the result of the inquiry.

Of these four hundred women, taken as they came, without special selection, about nine-tenths were found to belong to sixteen different regular small trades – namely, brushes, umbrellas, matchboxes, tennis-balls, ties, beads and braid, boots and shoes, cardboard boxes, artificial flowers, sacks, dolls, steel covering, tailoring, women's and children's clothing, shirts and fur-pulling. The rest, counting some thirty-three, worked at divers miscellaneous industries.

I. UMBRELLAS.

In this squalid series the first place – in class and pay – belongs to the umbrella trade, which is divided into covering – i.e., stitching together the covers – and finishing, which is fixing the covers on the frames. The former business is done more often than not in the factory; the latter – perhaps because the space required for working on a spread frame is too great for factory work – almost always at home. Considerable skill is required, and the women are of a superior class. The earning may be taken at from 2s. 6d. or 3s. a day to 5s. a week, while deductions for material run to 9d. a week. Parcels are heavy, and tram fare therefore must be allowed for. Export umbrellas, not much made in London, are worse paid for. In some departments the trade is seasonal.

II. FUR-PULLING.

At the other end of the scale come the fur-pullers – a deplorable tribe. No woman takes to this who is fit for anything else, and those who are driven to it by necessity are anxious to conceal the fact as far as possible from the prying eyes of the world. These women live in the utmost poverty and filth, in the back kitchens and attics of tenement dwellings in noisome courts and alleys. They work, eat, and sleep in an atmosphere thick with impalpable hairs and tainted with the sickly smell of the skins, everything around them coated with fur, and they themselves, in their sacklike dresses, ragged and open, looking scarcely more human than the animals whose skins they pluck, owing to the thick deposit of fur which covers them from head to foot and forces its way into their eyes, noses, and lungs. Their task is to remove with a plucking-knife the long hairs from rabbit skins, leaving only the soft silky down close to the skins. They earn about 1s. 1d. per day, and 4d. a week must be deducted for knives, &c. There is little difference in their condition or circumstances: all have sunk to the lowest depth of squalor and misery. They suffer from chronic asthma, and, of course, the rate of infant mortality is high. There would seem to be no remedy but to destroy the industry – at least as a home trade; the rooms might, at any rate, be registered and inspected as workshops.

III. TAILORING.

Mr. Sherwell has told us so much about the tailoresses of Soho, that it is hardly necessary to say more. The vice of this business is irregularity – slack work in winter. There are skilled hands doing the best work and living in comfort. But the conditions of the slop work are very different. The work lies all over the dirty room. The children stitch all day, and the wages, including the children's work, are about 1s. 3d. to 1s. 6d. a day, with deductions for thread and firing. Highest wages, 8s. 6d., lowest 9d.

IV. SHIRT-MAKING.

This trade much resembles tailoring; the work is lighter, but the "dress" in the cotton cloth is very disagreeable and unwholesome. Pay is very low – 7d. and 1s. a day, less 1d. for cotton. The better-paid work, on fine silk and wool materials, requires better home conditions to avoid soiling it.

V. CARDBOARD BOXES.

This trade varies very much in the nature of the work and rates of payment. Some boxes are made with glue or paste, others with needle and string. In the former case the cardboard has to be strengthened with paper at the corners, and sometimes wired: the lid is joined to the box, the box labelled, and the boxes tied up. "String work" has to be firmly sewn together with thread before being cornered and covered. The workers find their own glue, paste, thread, and string, which come to 1d. or 1½d. in the shilling. The best wages run to 3s. a day, the worst down to 6d. Children are very largely employed.

VI. BRUSH DRAWING.

This industry consists in drawing the fibre or bristles through the holes bored in the brush and fixing them by a wire, which ties them in the centre, and is then fastened at the back. Each row, when drawn, has to be trimmed with a pair of large shears, fastened to the table by a vice. The shears, vice, and finger-shields are supplied by the worker, all other materials by the shop. Shears cost some 18s., and need constant sharpening. If the woman has none, or has been obliged to pawn them, she has to have the trimming done at the shop, at a serious cost of time and money. The work is paid for according to the number of wires to be drawn, fibre brushes fetching 3½d. to 1s. a dozen, bristle brushes (not including tooth and nail brushes) from 1s. to 3s. 6d. It is difficult for the average worker to earn more than 6s. a week at fibre brushes; the average for bristles is perhaps 7s. to 8s. Tooth-brush drawers can hardly make more than 6s.

The work is clean and not unhealthy, but there is great risk of wounding the fingers with the wire. Foreign bristles have a "dressing" which brings a cough, especially to the children. It is, on the whole, very poor work, executed for small shops, and open to all the worst evils of home industry; an unskilled trade, in which supply exceeds demand.

VII. MATCHBOXES.

These workers seem to come next in wretchedness above the fur-pullers. They receive from five to eleven farthings per gross for making the boxes, subject to about 7 per cent. deduction for cost of materials, besides the expense of a fire to dry the boxes. Children help largely at this work. Severe poverty and much misery lie behind the figures in this return; the saddest cases being those of two old widows, living alone, of whom one, now slow at work, sets her day's earnings at 6d., while the other says she is often nearly starving. The average daily wage may perhaps be put as high as 1s. 4d., which includes the children. There is little variation in the rates of payment, and time is lost in waiting for work.

VIII. TIES.

This is a very variously paid and irregular business. Prices range from 6d. to 2d. a dozen, and wages from 3s. a day to 2s. a week, the great difference probably being due partly to shortages of work. It is a factory as well as a home industry; and even as a factory trade is not thought a good one. The workers seem to live far from the shops and lose time in fetching and carrying.

IX. RACKET TENNIS-BALL COVERING.

This is a Woolwich trade; rates of pay are uniform. In racket-balls work is regular; in tennis-balls wages are good, but the season very short – two or three months. "It is not a trade you can live by." Earnings (say), rackets 1s., tennis 2s., a day.

X. BEAD AND BRAID WORK.

The work and the wages both vary very widely. Changes of fashion as well as of season affect the business. There are periods of many years in which bead trimmings are hardly used at all; but just now there is a large demand. Complaints are made of time lost in fetching and waiting. It is not the worst paid work, but one worker says that it is only by neglecting everything that she can make 7s. a week. Earnings vary from about 3s., or even 3s. 6d., to 1s. or 6d. a day. Thread has to be found.

XI. BOOT AND SHOE MAKING.

Here, again, very wide differences appear both as to supply of work, rates of payment, and condition of the workers. Earnings run from 2s. 9d. a day, in one or two cases when work can be got, to 2½d. when it is very short: perhaps an average wage may be put at 1s. 9d., or something less. The women are mostly described as very respectable. The work is getting worse. One or two hours a day are lost in fetching.

XII. STEEL COVERING.

Here the pay and the workers are very poor. Earnings from 1s. 10d. to about 1s. a day. Work fairly regular.

XIII. DOLL-MAKING.

That is, stuffing and making-up dolls. The pay is better than in some trades, and earnings range from 2s. 8d. to 1s. a day; but German competition is pulling it down.

XIV. SACK-MAKING.

This is rough and heavy work. The sacks are stiff, and are stitched with a triangular needle and strong twine soaked in tar. The needle has to be passed through a lump of grease at each stitch. A metal shield is used on the palm of the hand. But the work is not badly paid, and 2s. a day can be earned on an average.

XV. ARTIFICIAL FLOWERS.

The best flowers, no doubt, are made in France, where the trade is an art, each specimen different from the others. This London work is in cheap and common flowers. Children are employed to a considerable extent, and the business is subject to fluctuations of season and fashion. Daily earnings from 2s. to 8d.; tools and some materials are generally found by the worker.

XVI. WOMEN'S AND CHILDREN'S CLOTHING.

This head, of course, covers a very large variety of employments, which however, all have one common melancholy note, that of "season trade." All branches are interrupted by long periods of slackness, usually in the winter, the hardest part of the year. One remark is that the organisation of such industries is out of the question. Some of the women mentioned propose to give the work up as not worth having. Hardly any one, indeed, can now live by hand-needlework, unless in a few cases of highly skilled work. There is serious competition from Ireland, where the cost of living in peasant homes is low. Cotton is always found by the worker. The highest earnings met with run from 2s. 6d. to 3s. a day, the lowest go down to 6d. or even less.

The miscellaneous trades comprise the making of bags, tassels and fringes, chair-caning and some other small manufacturers. Here and there may be found some women with a speciality, as, for example, a carman's wife who has inherited the business of carrying on some processes in making gold-beater's skin, and can earn 16s. a week for three days' work. But the mass are poverty-stricken and destitute, scratching together a very scanty wage with immense toil, and trying to live on 1s. a day or less.

It is cheering to know that the Government employees for Woolwich Arsenal are in a better condition. Work, though variable, is not so irregular;

wages are higher, and come to some 2s. 6d. a day, which is excellent for a woman's earnings. The children are not employed, to any great extent. The officials are not complained of; but some dislike the monthly payment; and it is said that the scarlet cordite bags hurt the eyes. These servants of the Government, however, have on the whole a good master.

The general result of the whole inquiry, as to wages, is as follows: Out of the 384 cases in which the earnings were ascertained, 126 – about one-third – earn 1s. a day or less; 127, from 1s. to 1s. 6d.; 66 from 1s. 6d. to 2s.; and only 67 over 2s.

As between home and factory work, the wage is very often the same; but the home worker has constantly to provide portions of plant or material; she has to fetch and carry the work and often to wait long for it; and when work is slack the factory hand gets the first chance.

But the most striking fact which has come out in the investigation is that the workers who are receiving the highest pay are often the wives of men in work, and who are therefore not so abjectly dependent on others or upon what they can make, and do not work so long hours; while the worst paid are often the spinsters and widows. Several reasons may be alleged for this. The widow is often old, and deficient in speed and endurance, while the spinster, in many cases, has failed to marry on account of weak health or infirmity. But it is probable also that the more prosperous and better-fed married woman is a more effective worker, and can accomplish more and better work than her less fortunate sister; can resist a reduction of rates, and command, from her greater efficiency, the better-paid work. Certainly it appears that a considerable proportion of women who avowedly work for supplementary profits earn more per hour, and sometimes at the same work and same rate, than those who grind for daily bread. If this be so, then the common view that supplementary wage-earning reduces the rate of pay can hardly be supported – a proposition which, if it were established, would tend to clear our ideas.

How long the starvation work is to go on is a question for the public conscience; for that schemes can be invented and means found for relieving it, if we are determined, there can be little doubt. But the object of this article is not to suggest a revolutionary, or even a remedial, industrial policy, but to set forth afresh, in some detail, the plain facts of the destitute life about us which we well know but fail to realise.

How to Deal with Home Work

There is no question of more importance to the wage earners of the country than that of home work. In reports of investigation into this subject undertaken by the Women's Industrial Council of London and the Scottish Council for Women's Trades, it has been shown, with convincing detail of actual cases, how home work very generally means insanitary work, how it leads to the reduction of wages all round, how it involves the excessive labour of children; and, as a result of their investigations, those Councils have drafted a Bill which has been introduced into Parliament in three sessions.*

POINTS OF THE BILL.

The Bill provides that, before work can be done in a living-room, a factory inspector must have examined the place and have given a certificate to the occupier that it is fit for being used as a workshop; but there is provision for a temporary certificate holding good for a month, so that workers may not be unjustly inconvenienced. Within the month the inspector must inspect, and it is provided that his visits therefore must not be more than six months apart. The certificate will be withdrawn if the inspector finds the place dirty, or overcrowded, or dangerous to health for any other reason. Employers giving out work to uncertified places are to be prosecuted.

The object of the Bill is to protect the public against the dissemination of disease and dirt by wearing apparel and other articles made in insanitary dwelling places, and to protect the workers themselves against unhealthy and vicious conditions over which they can exercise no control.

The Bill introduces no new standards of sanitation, and imposes no conditions beyond those already recognised by the Factories and Workshops, and the Public Health Acts. It has been drafted to correct many admitted failures in the administration of these Acts.

THE HOME WORKER TO BE LICENSED.

It proceeds upon the idea of licensing, subject to competent inspection.

1. The licences are to be granted *to individuals for specified premises, and for a limited period*, so as to prevent sub-letting and the sale of certificates.

---

* By Colonel Denny, John Burns, and others, 1902.

2. In the first instance the workpeople will have to apply for their certificates, but the method of the Bill reduces the trouble to a minimum, and this, the only responsibility placed upon the worker, is a very small matter, and will become of no importance when the Factory Inspectors' offices are properly organised for the work. The ease and regularity of the working of the system in Boston, Mass., and others of the American States, where it has been in force for some years, is very striking.* The Committee of the Women's Industrial Council has considered many alternative proposals, but the system finally adopted appears to be the most satisfactory, and the least likely to become a dead letter.

It may be noted that the principle of requiring a licence or certificate of fitness, in the case of certain factories and workshops, was strongly urged by the Royal Commission of Labour in their Report of 1894.

THE RESPONSIBILITY OF THE EMPLOYER.

3. The burden of responsibility is placed upon the employer, but in such a simple and straightforward way that he cannot reasonably object to it. In practice, the employer or his agent will have to see that every time an out-worker takes away material, he has in his possession a valid certificate. It has been suggested that the employer himself should get the certificate. In many cases this would simply mean that the worker interested would be his messenger. Moreover, the great trouble to which a man working for more than one employer would be put to get each of his employers to take out a certificate for him, would be more harassing than if he himself got his own certificate, and was enabled under it to work for as many employers as he liked. If employers took out the certificates, inspections would be multiplied needlessly where a worker was employed by several firms, and as one worker would be certified at various times to various employers, return visits, which are even more important than first inspections, would not be effectively carried out.

---

* The Industrial Commission of the United States reported last year in favour of the extension of the licensing law for home workers to all States where it is not yet in force.

The proposals to make the employers responsible for the sanitary state of their workpeople's dwelling houses, advocated by some people, should be specially guarded against, because:–

1. It could not be enforced.
2. If the housing of the outworkers is to be improved it is the house owner who must be got at.
3. Every attempt to induce employers to become house owners for their employees (as this proposal is) is pernicious.
4. What is wanted is to prevent the evil of insanitary home-work and not merely to punish for it when discovered.

WHO IS TO INSPECT?

The inspecting authority is the Factory, not the local Sanitary Inspector. This has been deliberately decided upon because the Sanitary Inspector is not sufficiently independent of local influence to be entrusted with this work; nor is his standard always so high as that of the Factory Inspector, nor his administration so uniform. The Women's Industrial Council opposed those clauses of the Factory Act of 1901 by which a greater share of the administration of the workshop clauses was put under the local authorities. Moreover, it considers that the cost of administering such a Bill as this should not be borne by the rates. To propose a further stringency in administering the provisions of the Public Health and Factory Acts, without raising this fundamental reason for some of their most disappointing failures, would be to shut our eyes to one of the most important questions which are ripening for solution.

WHAT IS EXPECTED OF THE BILL?

1. It will not put an end to homework: it will organise it. The genuine domestic worker suffers from the casual and nondescript nature of the work, and this is caused very largely by the fact that, like dock labour in the old days, the proportion of "casuals" working at home is great. When the certificate has been procured, the genuine home-worker will find a much more constant demand for his work, and, as a consequence, it will be possible to improve his conditions.
2. It will lead to co-operation between the Sanitary and Factory

Inspectors, which will result in a more efficient administration of the Public Health Acts, and the provision of better houses.

3. Although it does not touch hours of labour, by bringing the domestic workshop more directly under the eye of the Factory Inspector, it will lead to the enforcement of section 111 of the Factory Act of 1901 which is meant to control the excessive labour of children.

There are no complete statistics at present available as to the numbers of home-workers, but it will be noticed that the Bill is in no sense specially restrictive upon women's labour, and will apply to men and women alike, and probably in fairly equal numbers.

✳

Copies of the Bill can be had of the Women's Industrial Council, 19, Buckingham Street, Strand, W.C., 1½d. post free.

ALSO: Report of Investigation into Home Work industries in London. 6d., post free 7d.

Summary of Factory and Workshop Act, price 1d.

The Council's inquiry into married women's work

One of the most extensive inquiries undertaken by the Council was that into married women's work. Not published until 1915 because of the war and other factors, the investigation was begun in 1908. The final version included chapters on married women's work in London as well as in Yorkshire, Manchester, Liverpool, Newcastle, Reading and elsewhere. The introduction and the section on London were written by Clementina Black. In addition to containing information on the subject, the inquiry provides a chance to see something of the methods employed by the Council. The selections furnish us with the type of questions asked by the Council's investigators and a sample of the responses they received.

✳

Women's Industrial Council,
7, John Street, Adelphi, London, W.C.

25th September, 1908.

Dear Sir or Madam,

The Women's Industrial Council is initiating an enquiry into the effects of the industrial employment of married women. Nearly all the social questions of the day are affected by the fact of married women's labour, and, at present, no systematic enquiry into the subject has been made, and such information as exists is fragmentary and often inexact. A preliminary draft of the points to be investigated is enclosed, with a specimen case shewing the form which has been found most convenient for classification, and we are instructed to ask you to let us know whether you or your society would be willing to take any part in the investigation. The question is so large that the help of all those who have special knowledge in regard to any of its aspects will be needed, if the investigation is to be really useful. The Council proposes to publish the results in volume form and all co-operation will be fully acknowledged. As the expenses will be considerable, we shall be very grateful for any pecuniary contributions.

We are,
Yours faithfully,
CLEMENTINA BLACK, President.
H.D. PLAYER,
Hon. Sec. Investigation Committee.
L.WYATT-PAPWORTH, Secretary.

Name and Address of Enquirer
Date of Visit 190
Town or District to which the Report refers

Women's Industrial Council,
7, John Street, Adelphi, London, W.C.

Enquiry into the Industrial Employment of
Married Women and Widows.

A.–WORKER:–

Name and address (in full)

1. Married or Widowed
   Age
   Place of Work
   Town or Country Bringing-up
   Nationality
2. Occupation – (a) Regular
                 (b) Intermittent
                 (c) Before marriage
3. Reasons for Working
   Did the woman continue at her original work uninterrupted by marriage?
   or
   Did she return to it after a period?

B.– FAMILY AND HEALTH:–

1.–Rent and Number of Rooms–

   State of home $\left\{ \begin{array}{l} \text{Sanitation} \\ \text{Cleanliness} \\ \text{Furniture} \end{array} \right.$

   State of Children
2.–Number of Children alive–
   (a) Earning
   (Information should be given as to the nature of the occupation and the amount of the earnings of each child).

(b) Dependent

3.–Number of Children dead–

(a) Age at death

(b) Cause of death

(c) Had the mother been working during the year in which the child was born?

4.–Number of other dependents (if any)

5.–Arrangements for care of home and children during absence at work

6.–Effect of the work on the woman's health–

How long did she cease work at her confinements?

What provision was made (if any) to meet the expenses?

C.–WAGES:–

1. Woman's earnings

(Simple statements of average wages should not be accepted. Wherever possible, exact statements should be obtained of the earnings and hours worked over a series of consecutive weeks. Enquiry should also be made as to earnings in slack and busy seasons separately, and as to the length of these seasons. In the slack season of the woman's main occupation what other source of income or what subsidiary employment does she find?)

(a) Time wages

(b) Piece rates

(c) Average per week

(d) Number of hours worked and average payment per hour

(e) Have wages risen or fallen?

2. Husband's occupation and average weekly earnings

3. Total family income per week

From Husband

Wife

Children

Other dependents

Allotments

Lodgers

Thrift, Friendly Societies, etc.

Charity, Poor Law

4. Weekly budget.

(If the total family income is in excess of the weekly budget, what is done with the surplus?)

D.–REMARKS:–

E.–APPARENT ECONOMIC RESULTS:–

1. Does the fact that women work in the trade affect the men's wages?
2. Are women actually working in competition with men and tending to oust them, or is it the other way about?
3. Are married workers preferred to girls?
4. Is the women's work being more and more done by machinery?

F.–CHARACTERISTICS OF TRADE:–

1. Remarks–
   (a) Special characteristics of trade
   (b) Special characteristics of locality
2. Does the trade employ locally many
   (a) Men or boys
   (b) Married women and widows
   (c) Girls?
      (Give approximate numbers.)
3. Is the occupation healthy?
4. Is the trade organised?

G.–LEGISLATION & GENERAL:–

1. Is legislation on the subject of married women's work desirable or not?
2. Legislative Proposals.
   (a) English.
   (b) Foreign.
3. Schemes for the amelioration of Infantile Conditions.
   (a) English.
   (b) Foreign.
4. Schemes for Maternity Insurance.
   References to sources of information on any of these subjects will be welcome contributions towards the bibliography of the subject.

Women's Industrial Council,
7, John Street, Adelphi, London, W.C.

Hints to Investigators.

The following notes are in the character not so much of directions as of suggestions, and are the outcome of prolonged (and often trying) experience in the work of investigation and of drawing up reports.

The report of each separate case should be written on half-sheets of paper about 7 in. by 4½ in., each heading (such as A., worker; B., family and health) occupying one separate sheet, or more than one if necessary.

Papers should be fastened together with paper fasteners not with pins.

The first page of each report should bear –

(a) The name and address of the Investigator.

(b) The date.

(c) The town or district to which the report refers.

The name and address of the woman should be repeated on the top right-hand corner of each sheet. This is essential as the pages have to be separated for classification and tabulation.

In making visits to workers, it will generally be found unwise to write down any notes while actually on the premises. A rough book is convenient for noting answers immediately after leaving, and these should be written out at the earliest possible moment.

Reports should be as lifelike and complete as possible. Details that seem, in the individual case, unimportant, become significant when they recur again and again. Thus, the appearance of good or bad health, cheerfulness or the reverse, are points worth noting; and so are any little details that may be given of family history in the previous generation. Too much detail is preferable to too little.

SPECIMEN CASE

A.   1. Mrs. O'Rooney, 108, Perpendicular Buildings, Tiger Court, Drury Lane.

Married. 41. House, also Market. Country. Irish.

2. Shirt finishing. Occasionally shelling peas.

(a) Only works at shirt when her husband is either partially or wholly out of work. Shells peas at Covent Garden in the season.

(b) Intermittent.

(c) Worked in a Laundry.

3. No. She gave up the Laundry at the birth of first child, and has not returned to it.

B. 1. 9s. Three rooms and scullery. Sanitary condition good. Cleanliness leaves much to be desired. Furniture old, and much too large for habitation.

Children apparently healthy, but neither clean nor tidy.

2. Five. (a) Girl, 14; just gone to factory; 4s. a week; gives mother 2s. 6d.

Boy, 13; goes round with milkman; 5s.; gives mother 2s.

(b) Three; baby of a year, girl of 6, and boy of 10.

3. Four. (a) Two died at less than a fortnight old; one at 3; one at 8.

(b) One baby died in a fit; one was born weakly, and died on the third day; child of 3 died of measles; boy of 8 run over by motor omnibus.

(c) Yes; but not continuously.

4. Grandmother, aged 84; has pension of 4s. 6d., and lives with this family.

5. Works at home. Takes baby with her when she goes out to shell peas, or leaves it with grandmother.

6. Says her eyes have been weakened by strain of working by gas light. Was sewing shirts, in bed, when the last baby (born in winter) was three days old. Worked up to the day of the birth. No provision on the last occasion.

C. 1. (a) None of the work is paid by time.

(b) Shirts 3d. or 8d. per dozen. Unable to learn the exact rate for shelling peas. Says she "has often made 6d. for a morning, leaving off before 11."

(c) About 8s.

(d) In bad times has worked fourteen hours. Says she can get five dozen of cheaper shirts finished in a long day; but probably children help. This would make 1s. 3d. per day, less cotton, which she provides.

(e) Says that rates were just double what they are now when she used to help her elder sister do the work, about 15 years ago.

2. Covent Garden Porter. Sometimes has earned as much as 45s. in the week. More often 30s. There are long slack times in which he earns no more than 10s.

3. Earnings of husband vary from 10s. to about 42s., average about 27s.; wife earns about 7s. 4d. net when he is earning little; daughter earns 4s., keeps 1s. 6d.; son earns 5s., keeps 3s.; grandmother has weekly income of 4s. 6d. Average income somewhere about 35s.

4. Weekly budget is only exceeded in prosperous times. Excess seems to pay debts incurred in bad times.

D.   Mrs. O'Rooney is a stout, cheerful, slatternly woman, who may occasionally drink. Husband has bouts of drinking, but not frequently. The eldest boy and girl very intelligent and good looking.

E.   1. Men do not work in the trade, except as cutters.
2. Neither one nor the other.
3. No; but girls do not seem to do shirt finishing at home.
4. Buttonholes are being done by machinery; but the bars at the end of them are still made by hand.

F.   1. (a) Shirt finishing at home has ceased to be a trade that affords a livelihood.
(b) Locality is rough and crowded; rents high. Market porters must live near to market.
2. (a) Perhaps two men as cutters; not boys.
(b) Not very many. This woman got work through her sister, who lives north of Holborn.
(c) A few girls work in shirt factories; but only one factory is in this district.
Quite impossible to give numbers.
3. Not in itself unhealthy. An unpleasant, and probably unhealthy, fluff comes from cheap flannelette shirts.
4. No; though a Union exists.

G.   1. Legislation does not seem needed to regulate the work of this woman.
The fixing of a minimum wage for shirt makers might help her.

2.
3. } No information on these points.
4.

October, 1908.

Council lectures

The Council's activities were wide ranging. In addition to the investigation of trades, its members gave lectures on numerous subjects at girls' clubs; branches of different organizations, such as the Women's Co-operative Guild and the National Union of Women Workers; to church associations, including the CSU; to Sunday associations; political clubs; and to working men's and women's clubs. In addition, it helped arrange lectures on women's issues at Bedford College and King's College for Women. The first selection is a description of the Council's lecture series from its Annual Report of 1906–7. The lecture list is for 1907–8. This is followed by a blurb which appeared in *WIN* of September 1906 and summarizes the categories of lectures sponsored by the Council. The final selection in this section is the syllabus for a course at King's College arranged by the Council which began on 24 January 1907.*

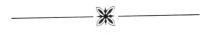

Women's Industrial Council lectures, 1907–8

A large number of Speakers are willing to give their services free for lectures, talks and debates, both for propaganda and to add to the income of the Council. Travelling expenses must, however, be paid, and a donation in proportion to the Society's means must be sent to the Council. Applications from Societies possessing *no funds at all* will be ˙considered on their merits.

---

* Lectures, 1907–8, in Thirteenth Annual Report 1906–7; The New Lecture List, *WIN*, **36** (September 1906), p. 563; Syllabus for King's College Lecture, Twelfth Annual Report, 1905–6.

All applications for lectures should be sent to the Secretary, Women's Industrial Council, 7, John Street, Adelphi, Strand, W.C. All applications must be accompanied by a postage fee of one shilling (in Post Office Order or stamps), or half-a-crown, when more than three lectures are to be arranged.

Particulars of the lectures desired should not be given in the form of a long letter, but on a separate sheet of paper and under the following numbered heads.

(1) Name and address of Secretary.
(2) Name and address of lecture room.
(3) Day, date and hour.
(4) Size and nature of audience.
(5) The number of the lecture desired.
(6) Alternative numbers and dates.

It is advisable that at least a fortnight's notice should be given.

As soon as a lecture has been arranged, the Secretary will send the name and address of the Speaker, to whom full details of place, date, hour, mode of transit, nature of audience, etc., should be sent at once. It is advisable to send the Speaker a post card reminder on the day before the lecture.

Travelling expenses should be paid to the Speaker at the time, and it is expected that the donation will be sent to the Secretary at the office before the last lecture of the series.

LECTURE LIST

No. of Lecture.	Lecturer	Subject
1.	Miss Adler	The Children in our Elementary Schools
2.	"	The Special Schools of London
3.	"	Skilled Trades for Working Girls
4.	"	Trade Schools for Girls
5.	"	The Employment of Children Act
6.	"	Separate Courts of Justice for Children
7.	Miss L. Ashe	Character as a Cause of Poverty
8.	"	Thrift
9.	Mrs. M. Beer, M.A.	Apprenticeship and Skilled Employment
10.	Mrs. Bunting	Infant Mortality

No. of Lecture.	Lecturer	Subject
11.	Mrs. Bunting	The Care of Poor Law Girls
12.	"	Domestic Service
13.	"	The White Slave Traffic
14.	Miss E. Ormiston Chant	Temperance Work in Girls' Clubs
15.	" ...	The Work of the B.W.T.A.
16.	" ...	The Road to health and how to walk it
17.	" ...	Breathing and Physical Culture
18.	Mrs. J.W. Davis	First aid
19.	"	Home Nursing
20.	"	The Home
21.	"	The Mother
22.	"	The Infant
23.	"	The Child
24.	Mrs. Eates	Some Skilled Trades for Working Girls
25.	"	The Apprenticeship charities of London
26.	Mr. G.P. Gooch, M.P. ...	Sweating
27.	" ...	Foreign Methods of dealing with the unemployed
28.	Dr. L. Haden Guest ...	Diet Reform and Poverty
29.	" ...	Diet and Efficiency
30.	" ...	The Hygiene of Factory Production
31.	" ...	Dangers of the Employment of Women
32.	Miss Daisy Hollington, B.A.	Temperance (various aspects)
33.	" ...	Women's Suffrage
34.	Mrs. Colin Lamont, A.R.S.I.	The Body and its functions
35.	" ...	The Air we breathe
36.	" ...	The Food we eat
37.	" ...	How to grow a Healthy Baby
38.	" ...	Health in the Home
39.	" ...	The Health of the Community
40.	Dr. Lydia Leney	The Care of the Eyes in Childhood and Adult Life
41.	"	The Decline of the Birth-rate and Infant Mortality
42.	Miss C.P. Lewis	The Establishment of Employment Bureaux in Clubs
43.	Mr. J.R. MacDonald, M.P.	The Labour Laws of Australasia
44.	" ...	Women and Unemployment
45.	" ...	Why I am not in favour of Wages Boards
46.	Mrs. J.R. MacDonald ...	Labour Laws in our Colonies

No. of Lecture.	Lecturer	Subject
47.	Mrs. J.R. MacDonald	Married Women as Wage Earners
48.	"	The Problem of Home Work
49.	"	Day Trade schools for Girls
50.	"	The Disgrace of Child Labour
51.	Mrs. H.W. Macrosty	The Minimum Wage
52.	Mr. Albert Mansbridge	The Education of Workpeople
53.	"	The Schools of England
54.	"	The Workers' Educational Association
55.	"	Education and Working Women
56.	Miss M.E. Marshall	Thrift, or looking Ahead
57.	"	Charity
58.	Mrs. Meyerstein	Children after School Age: their difficulties and how to help them
59.	"	How best to help the Poor
60.	Hon. L.H. Montagu	Recreation and Religion
61.	"	The Happiness of Work
62.	"	The Training of the Club Leader
63.	"	The Relation of the Club to the Workshop and Home
64.	Mr. H.T. Muggeridge	The True Principles of Municipal Indebtedness
65.	"	The Labour Movement and its Relation to Progress
66.	"	Socialism and Women
67.	"	The Housing Question
68.	Miss Mary Muir	Women and Socialism
69.	"	Women as Politicians
70.	"	Sweated Industries
71.	"	Educational Ideals
72.	"	Feeding of School Children
73.	"	Medical Inspection of School Children
74.	Mrs. Thomas Okey	The Constitution of the House of Commons
75.	"	Domestic Service: the Mistress and the Maid
76.	Miss Parton	Children in different Lands
77.	"	The Progress of Child Legislation
78.	"	The Work of the N.S.P.C.C.
79.	Miss S.R. Perkins	The Employment of Barmaids
80.	"	Openings for Women in our Colonies
81.	Miss Penrose Philp	How to help Poor Law Children
82.	"	The Emigration of Poor Law Children
83.	"	Separate courts of Justice for Children

No. of Lecture.	Lecturer	Subject
84.	Mr. E.H. Pickersgill, M.P.	The Minimum Wage
85.	"	Prison Reform
86.	Mrs. Pickford	Why sign the Total Abstinence Pledge
87.	"	How Girls can help the Temperance cause
88.	Miss Mildred Ransom ...	Women's Suffrage
89.	" ...	Women in Local Government
90.	" ...	Women in Business
91.	" ...	Laws of Health
92.	Mr. Frederick Rogers ...	Old Age Pensions
93.	Miss F.L. Staff	Towards the Co-operative Commonwealth
94.	"	Brotherhood in Business
95.	"	Brotherhood in Daily Life
96.	"	International Brotherhood
97.	"	Competition and the Way Out
98.	Mrs. Styer	First Aid
99.	"	Hygiene
100.	"	Home Nursing
101.	"	Ventilation
102.	"	The Maintenance of Health
103.	Miss Alice Wadmore, A.R.S.I.	School Hygiene
104.	" ...	Sanitation in the Home
105.	" ...	Ambulance
106.	" ...	Nursing

Lectures will be arranged, if required, on the work of the Women's Industrial Council, the Association of Trained Charwomen, and the work of Girls' Clubs.

Lectures on Hygiene, Nursing, Sanitation, Thrift subjects other than those specified will be arranged as asked for.

An additional list is kept in manuscript at the office, and societies not finding precisely what they require in the above list are asked to communicate with the Secretary.

THE NEW LECTURE LIST

The Lecture List has been revised and reprinted. It is now too long to include in full in the *News*, but anyone can have copies of it on application at the office. There are 35 lecturers with 111 lecture titles, embracing, among many others, the following subjects:—

The Home.— Marriage. Motherhood. Care of the Infant. Infantile Mortality. Causes of National Deterioration. Domestic Economy. First Aid. Nursing.

Education.— Care of the Young Child. Simple Ailments. State Feeding of School Children. Employment of Children. Children's Courts. Skilled Trades. Apprenticeship.

Economics.— Thrift. Benefit Societies. Wise Spending and Wise Saving.

Sanitation.— Alcoholism and Temperance. Public Health Acts. Hygiene. Care of Health. Consumption. Vegetarianism. Children's Dress. Garden Cities.

Social Subjects.— The Colonies. Old Age Pensions. Minimum Wage. Work of the L.C.C. The Education Authority. Unemployed. Farm Colonies. Labour Movement. Municipalism. Milk Supply. Socialism. Women's Work. Emigration.

Industrial Subjects.— Skilled Trades. Home Industries. Work of Barmaids. Citizenship. Girls' Clubs. Talks on Trades.

SYLLABUS, KING'S COLLEGE LECTURES

The course arranged for King's College for Women begins on January 24th, 1907. The syllabus is given below. The attention of members of the Council and their friends is directed to this course, in the hope that they will do their best to make this opportunity of extending the Council's sphere of influence and work a really great success.

THE RELATION OF THE STATE TO WOMEN'S WORK
Thursday, 3 p.m., beginning January 24th.

Lecturers nominated by the Women's Industrial Council.

Lent Term

1. *The Economic Position of the Woman Wage-Earner*. B. Kirkman Gray, Esq., F.S.S.–Statistics of women's wages in the nineteenth century–Has legislation affected women's wages?–Other causes affecting wages–Comparison between different trades–Foreign countries.

2. *The History of Legislation affecting Women in Trade and Industries*. Miss B.L. Hutchins.–A century of Factory Acts–Robert Owen–Shaftesbury–The Act of 1901–Inspection: Comparison with English colonies; with foreign countries–Suggestions for legislation.

3. *The Training of the Worker*. Mrs. H.A. Oakeshott.–Apprenticeship abuses, disuse, Revival. Work of the committees–Technical classes in polytechnics–The new trade classes and technical day schools of the L.C.C.–Lessons from other countries–Prospects.

4. *Organisation for Women Workers*. Miss MacArthur.–Clubs–Co-operative guilds–Benefit societies–Trade unions–Strikes, &c.

5. *The Present Position of Women in Factories*. Miss L.H. Montagu.–The life and ways of the girl of to-day in the factory and workshop–Marriage and infantile mortality from the industrial standpoint–The employment of children as it affects industrial conditions–Holidays–Improvements that might be made.

6. *The Present Position of Women Home-Workers*. Mrs. Beer, M.A.–Life of the home-worker–Tendency of prices to fall–Conditions of trade–Sweating–Comparison with other countries–Proposed legislation to remedy worst evils–Recent legislation in New York.

7. *The Present Position of Women Shop Assistants*. Miss Bondfield.–The conditions of life–Truck–The living-in system–Recent legislation–Reforms.

8. *The Present Position of Women in Domestic Service*. Miss Clementina Black.–The past–Existing conditions–Possible reforms–Registries–New powers of the L.C.C., &c.

Applications for tickets should be made to the Principal, King's College for Women, 13, Kensington Square, W.

The Clubs' Industrial Association

The Clubs Industrial Association (CIA) was founded by the Council to organize club life in London. The following selection appeared in the Council's Annual Report of 1906–7* and describes the objects and activities of the Association. It also illustrates the dual role the Council saw for working girls' education.

CLUBS' INDUSTRIAL ANNUAL REPORT, 1906–7

DEFINITION OF THE CLUBS' INDUSTRIAL ASSOCIATION

The Clubs' Industrial Association is an Association of Leaders and Representative Members of Working Girls' Clubs who are bound together in order to study and, when opportunity arises, to improve the lives of Working Girls.

WHY THE CLUBS' INDUSTRIAL ASSOCIATION WAS FORMED

During working hours girls have no time or opportunity to study the Laws enacted for their benefit, and unless strengthened by association with other workers, they are afraid to use their own rights, even when they understand them. The founders of the Clubs' Industrial Association realising these facts and, believing that the Clubs are the best medium for influencing the Industrial lives of girls, appealed to Club Leaders to take their share in the educational work of spreading a knowledge of Factory Laws and strengthening the sense of responsibility among workers. The workers were themselves asked to support good employers by combating the unfair competition of bad employers, who prospered by the infringement of the Factory Laws. The formation of the Clubs' Industrial Association was encouraged by the Inspectors themselves, who felt that the co-operation of the workers was necessary, especially as the field of inspection is so vast and their numbers so small.

OBJECTS OF CLUBS' INDUSTRIAL ASSOCIATION

1. To affiliate Working Girls' Clubs together, with a view to studying

---

* WIC, Thirteenth Annual Report, 1906–7.

Industrial Law, doing Investigation Work, reporting infringements of Factory Laws, *via* the Women's Industrial Council, to the Home Office.

2. To unite Clubs in different districts of London by making them realize the common aims of good citizenship.

3. To stimulate the sense of responsibility among wage-earners (*a*) towards themselves; (*b*) towards their employers; (*c*) towards each other; (*d*) towards posterity.

METHODS OF THE CLUBS' INDUSTRIAL ASSOCIATION WORKING THROUGH AN EXECUTIVE OF CLUB LEADERS ELECTED BY AFFILIATED CLUBS

1. Organising three Social Meetings annually at 8, Dean Street, Oxford Street, when lectures are given on Industrial, Social, or Educational questions and friendly discussion and intercourse are encouraged. To these Meetings Club Leaders and Representative Members, not necessarily members of the Club Committees, are invited.

2. Organising lectures or series of lectures to Club Leaders on the systematic study of Industrial questions.

3. Arranging lectures in clubs to which representatives of neighbouring clubs are invited.

4. Organising Citizen Classes (held weekly, fortnightly or monthly) in various Clubs, to which neighbouring Clubs are generally invited to send delegates. At these Classes subjects of Industrial, Social or Political import are discussed. For example, in some instances, the newspaper is studied week by week, and the girls thus become interested in the general life of the community. Some Club Leaders prefer to take an Industrial subject like Trades Unionism and explain its history and possibilities in a series of "talks," others describe the manner in which London is governed, and attend with their members a County Council or Borough Council Meeting to give practical illustration to their teaching. A Syllabus on the British Empire has been drawn up by Miss Wileman for use in Citizen Classes.

5. Forming Citizen Committees in different districts of London for doing simple investigation work. These Committees are generally officered by Club Members and include representatives of several clubs.

6. Reporting cases of illegal practice in Workshops and Factories to the

Home Office; the existence of the illegality having been first carefully verified by responsible enquirers.

7. Circulating in Clubs tracts on Factory Laws and other literature, with a view to increasing members' knowledge of Industrial Law.

8. Giving voice to the necessity for improvements in the Industrial conditions of Workshop and Factory life, by means of petitions, &c.

WHAT THE CLUBS' INDUSTRIAL ASSOCIATION HAS DONE

1. It has affiliated 37 Working Girls' Clubs (affiliation subscription of 1s. each to be sent to the Hon. Sec.) and has got into touch with about 50 others.

2. Besides organising regular business and social meetings and arranging a number of local lectures, it has established a Citizen Committee in South London and encouraged the formation of Citizen Classes at Clubs in the North, West, West Central and East districts of London.

3. The affiliated Clubs signed a petition for the increase of sanitary accommodation in Workshops and Factories and circulated Miss Black's Rhyme of the Factory Act and other publications of the Women's Industrial Council.

4. The Association has safeguarded the interests of working girls by reporting cases of infringement of Factory and Sanitary Laws through a central organization, and by acquainting affiliated clubs with the existence of the Indemnity Fund established by the Industrial Law Committee, and by allowing them to benefit, if necessary, by the free legal advice offered by Messrs. Black and Garnett, Hon. Solicitors to the Women's Industrial Council.

WHAT THE CLUBS' INDUSTRIAL ASSOCIATION HOPES TO DO

1. To affiliate a large proportion of London Clubs, and to establish branches of the Association in the Provinces.

2. To organize more lectures, and to develop all branches of citizenship work in various districts of London.

3. To develop all the other possibilities of educational work which it has formulated.

The Officers of the Clubs' Industrial Association earnestly appeal to the readers of this leaflet to make known in Clubs the aims and objects of their organization. They believe that, through education in Industrial and Social subjects, English Working Girls will become more useful citizens. Their horizon being enlarged, they will be more awake to their corporate responsibilities, more desirous of achieving efficiency as workers, and more capable of self-sacrifice for the welfare of the State. They will be better equipped for wifehood and motherhood, inasmuch as their sense of proportion will be quickened through interest in the important issues of life and through the recognition of their duty to the coming generation of workers.

'Newspaper classes' for girls' clubs

One of the objects of the Association was 'to widen the intellectual outlook of working girls'. It was hoped to achieve this, in part, through 'newspaper and citizenship classes'. What follows are notes on special subjects compiled by the CIA for the use of club leaders in these classes. These suggestions are from 1908 and 1909.*

✳

WOMEN'S SUFFRAGE.

Introduction.—Find out what the Class already knows or has heard about the subject. This information will probably be very crude and incomplete, but can be used as a starting point for the lesson, and can be made to lead on to the question of—

1. The meaning and significance of the "Vote."

Illustrate this by reference to a simple state of society; also how the possession of a vote would affect those who suffered under a grievance.

---

* From Clubs Industrial Association, *Suggestions for Newspaper Classes Held in Girls' Clubs* (1908), and Women's Industrial Council, *Newspaper and Citizenship Classes and How to Hold them With Specimen Lessons* (1909).

2. How men obtained the Parliamentary Franchise. Description of the struggles for it.

3. Present conditions on which it is held by men.

4. The Women's movement; how it arose; recent agitation.

5. Reasons why women need the vote; specially referring to the industrial condition of women workers.

6. Methods of different sections of the Women's movement.

N.B.—For this lesson pamphlets, leaflets, etc., should be obtained beforehand from the Suffrage Societies, and should be distributed after the Class.

A Debate should, if possible, be arranged later.

PROBLEM OF UNEMPLOYMENT AMONG WOMEN.

Introduce by referring to the prominence and importance of the subject—how it affects women wage -earners. But when talked about, it is generally men's want of work which is discussed and for which remedies are proposed. What about unemployed women and girls? It is just as bad for them; often worse. The greater number of women do not work for wages, but look after the home, and the menfolk, and the children, and so earn a share of the menfolk's wages. But, according to census figures, nearly five million women and girls do wage-earning work in England and Wales.

Describe roughly the kinds of work—domestic service largest occupation; textile mills and factories, especially in Lancashire and Yorkshire; clothing trades, miscellaneous factories, workrooms, shops, etc. Many of these suffer from unemployment. Causes (*a*) Season trades have slack time every year for many of their workers. (*b*) Times of bad trade. (*c*) Changes of fashion. All these make it worse occasionally. (*d*) Unemployment amongst men often makes that amongst women worse, for two reasons, (1) the wives of unemployed men do work themselves, laundry, cleaning, etc., instead of giving it to others to do, and (2) compete in already crowded labour markets, throwing others out of work.

How unemployed women suffer. For girls and unmarried women, stoppage of work may mean great privation. Some living at home may not be altogether dependent on their own earnings, but many are, and many help to keep the home together, so that those dependent on them suffer. The sufferings of wives and widows with families dependent on their earnings, when they cannot get work which brings in wages, is almost too cruel to bear thinking of; but thousands of women have to live through that anguish.

Special circumstances of women. Women suffer, on the whole, *more* than men when out of work since:–

(*a*) Their wages are lower when in work and leave less wages for saving against a slack time.

(*b*) There are comparatively few women in trade unions, and those unions which exist are scarcely ever strong enough to give unemployed benefit.

Possible remedies. The causes of unemployment are so varied and the evil so deeply rooted, that no one remedy can meet the difficulty. But we can see certain lines along which to work.

In any attempts made to help the unemployed, unemployed women must be included.

(1) Distress committees should have special sub-committees to deal with women applicants. Where these applicants cannot be found work by means of Labour Exchanges and Employment Registries, special work should be provided as is done for men. In London, workrooms for making clothing have been at work, and have helped hundreds of women to tide over evil times. Manchester, Glasgow, and other places are establishing workrooms, too. In some cases, contracts have been obtained from Guardians and other public bodies. The difficulty of selling the clothes so as not to throw others out of work may be met by giving them, perhaps at cost price, to school committees, or distributing them to the unemployed themselves through Distress Committees.

(2) The Women's Industrial Council, and others interested in the problem, suggest that country colonies should be established for unemployed women, but this has not yet been tried.

(3) Other remedies must be more indirect. Abolition of child labour, better education of worker to enable them to do more skilled and various kinds of work.

Get up-to-date particulars from Central (Unemployed) Body, Temple Chambers, Temple Avenue, E.C.

(4) Better organisation of workers to ensure against slackness.

(5) Better organisation of our industrial system to avoid waste and misery of unemployment.

(6) Recognition of the fact that a woman with young children or other helpless dependents should be free to give full attention to her home, and that if there is no other bread winner in the family, the public authority should give adequate maintenance to herself and those dependent on her without any taint of pauperism and without breaking up the home as long as she keeps it properly.

The Council deals with Unemployment

Unemployment

Almost since its founding, the Council had shown interest in the plight of unemployed women. For example, in 1898, it created the Association of Trained Charwomen. This Association attempted to provide a systematic method of finding employment for what the Council considered 'one of the most helpless classes in the community'. It was a relatively small organization but for those it could help, it provided a week's thorough training in household work followed by membership in the Association which entitled women to character references. The following advertisement appeared frequently in the *WIN* and described briefly the Association's efforts.*

The Association of

Trained Charwomen,

Caretakers, Supply Servants, Laundry
Women, Jobbing Dressmakers,
Upholsteresses, Carpet Menders, and
Women for Odd Jobs.

* From *WIN*, **34** (March 1906), p. 546.

The Association was established by the Women's Industrial Council in 1898.

It is not a Registry Office. Registration as an Employment Bureau under the L.C.C. has been applied for.

LETTERS, enclosing stamped and addressed envelope for reply, should be sent to Miss Potter, Hon. Sec., A.T.C., 7, John Street, Adelphi, Strand, W.C.

POST OFFICE ORDERS should be crossed, and made payable to Miss F. Potter, at Southampton Street, Strand.

HOURS FOR INTERVIEWS: 10-30 a.m. to 3-30 p.m. The office is closed on Saturdays, but letters are attended to as usual.

TO EMPLOYERS

The A.T.C. consists of a large staff of women, all of whom are thoroughly recommended from personal experience for honesty, sobriety, general character, and knowledge of their work. The charwomen are women who have been in good service, and who, when necessary, have been further trained under a certificated teacher of Domestic Economy. The jobbing dressmakers and others are workers of skill and experience, who have been selected and tested with great care. The A.T.C. is thus able to offer to employers in every district of London and neighbourhood, assistance in all domestic emergencies. Compliance with demands under 48 hours' notice cannot be guaranteed. If shorter notice is given, an extra shilling for telegraph charges should be sent, and a worker can then usually be supplied within a few hours.

Terms: 6d. for an engagement of a week or less; 1s. up to a month. For supply servants, needlewomen, and upholsteresses, the fees for the week and the month are doubled. Amounts up to one shilling should be sent in half-penny stamps. Fee for permanent engagements by arrangement with the Hon. Sec.

A subscription of 5s. covers all engagements with every class of worker for a year.

THE COUNCIL'S SCHEME FOR UNEMPLOYED WOMEN

The Council was also instrumental in bringing the issue of unemployed women to the public eye in the early part of this century, partly by a letter-writing campaign to public officials in London. The following letter was addressed to the Central (Unemployed) Body for London, created in 1905 under the Unemployed Workmen Act. The same letter had been sent to the Central Body's predecessor in 1904. The suggestions in the letter formed the basis of the plans undertaken or considered by the Women's Work Committee of the Central Body in the succeeding years. The Central Body operated three sewing workrooms in the Metropolis and attempted to set up a farm colony for women, based on the Council's suggestions.

Women's Industrial Council.
7, John Street, Adelphi, Strand, W.C.

December, 1905

MEMORANDUM ADDRESSED TO THE CENTRAL COMMITTEE AND LOCAL DISTRESS COMMITTEES APPOINTED TO DEAL WITH UNEMPLOYMENT IN LONDON.

The Women's Industrial Council, having evidence that there is special distress from unemployment amongst women and girls in various districts and various trades in London, wishes to draw the attention of the Distress Committees to the serious way in which this affects women and girls who are dependent upon their own earnings. We ask the Distress Committees to give special consideration to the problem of meeting the needs of such women and girls, and would make the following suggestions towards practical help:—

1. That in all notices to the unemployed, forms of application, &c., issued by the Committees, it should be specifically stated that women who are dependent on their own earnings may apply as well as men, and that their cases will receive careful attention.

2. That wherever it is possible for the local authorities to undertake extra

work which women can do, *e.g.*, cleaning, upholstery, needlework, &c., this should be provided.

3. That where the local authorities are unable to provide employment for women applicants, either through the Labour Bureaux or by special work under (2), these should be referred to the Central Committee to be dealt with.

4. That on the Land Colony or Colonies in connection with the Distress Committees, a portion of the Colony should be set apart for women.

(a) To be employed in the necessary laundry work, mending or making of clothes, and cooking for the workers.

(b) To take part in some of the lighter work on the land.

(c) To be trained in gardening, dairy work, or poultry farming.

5. That for women and girls whose home circumstances prevent their moving to a Labour Colony outside London, one or more centres should be opened where they may obtain continuous employment for wages at making clothes; and that any garments made by them should not be sold, but given through responsible and experienced social workers to those in need.

6. That where remunerative work cannot be provided, a small maintenance grant might be given, on condition that those receiving it should attend domestic economy, or other suitable classes, at some Polytechnic or Technical Institute. This might specially apply to those willing to enter domestic service. The possibility might also be considered of teaching trades at present not largely followed in England.

In making these suggestions, the Women's Industrial Council has tried to carry out the principle upon which it believes the Distress Committees are working – that work given to the unemployed should be specially organised, so that they do not displace other workers, and that any work undertaken should be really useful.

ISHBEL ABERDEEN, *President.*
L. WYATT PAPWORTH, *Gen. Sec.*

Clementina Black

One of the founders of the Council and its third President, Clementina Black, had at one time been a writer of romantic fiction. Obviously she did not reject her literary bent and applied her skills to writing about social problems in numerous articles and books about women's work. She also continued to write poetry. As the Fifth Annual Report (1898–9) of the Council claimed, 'The farmer has his Hesiod and his Virgil, the factory lass has now her Clementina Black.' The poem reprinted below, 'The Rhyme of the Factory Acts', was meant to convey the essence of the Factory and Workshop Acts which applied to women and girls and was intended for distribution in working girls' clubs.

'THE RHYME OF THE FACTORY ACTS'.

Definitions.

In factories, machines must go
By steam or gas or power; if no
Such power is used, the place will be
A workshop, whether two or three
Or hundreds work, or only one;
In every place where work is done
(Except at home) the law has made
A set of rules to be obeyed.

Space.

In every sort of working place
For every soul must be a space
Of air (two-fifty cubic feet)
To keep the workroom fresh and sweet
In overtime the space is more,
The hundreds then go up to four.

Authorities.

The factory inspectors do
For factories and laundries too,
If these are worked by steam; if not,
The local Councils on the spot
Through their inspectors have to see
That things are as they ought to be;
In workshops too the rule is theirs,
And they must see that doors and stairs
Or fire escapes are well supplied,
Lest workers sh[o]uld be burned or fried.

Who is a
Child, &c.

Between eleven and fourteen
People are 'children,' and between
That and eighteen 'young persons,' then
They count as women or as men.

Cleaning
Machinery.

You must not put a child to clean,
While it is going, a machine;
The cleaning of mill-gearing, too,
Young folk and women must not do,
Unless it's still, nor work between
The moving parts of a machine.

Fencing.

Hoists, fly-wheels, races, gearing, each
Must be fenced round, or out of reach.

Hours.

Or working hours we next must speak
Which may be, on five days a week,
For women and young people, these:
From six to six, or, if you please,
Seven to seven, eight to eight,
With mealtimes out—but not so late
On Saturdays, when work is o'er
At two, or three, or else at four.

Meals.

For mealtimes there must always be
An hour before the clock strikes three;
For tea another half is due
Before the working day is through;

And on the shorter Saturday
There's half an hour for food or play.

Length of Work
at one spell.

No woman at her work must take
More than five hours without a break.

Non-textile
and textile
factories.

These are the hours in general. In
Mills where the women weave and spin
Their time is shorter at the loom
And longer in the dining room.

Meals for textile
workers.

Two hours their meals must occupy
As every working day goes by;
And one hour of the two must be
At some time earlier than three.

Spell of work for
textile workers.

Nor must they work a spell of more
Than one half hour beyond the four.

Saturdays for
textile workers.

While work on Saturdays is ceased
One whole hour earlier at least;
But in a mill where work's begun
At six, it must leave off at one;
And out of that, the whirring wheels
Must stop an hour complete for meals.
Or if there's shorter eating time
At half past twelve the bell must chime;
At two, of course, or half past one,
When work at seven was begun.

Particulars
Clause.

Besides all this, in many a trade
Where textiles or where clothes are made
Particulars of pay must be
Placed on a placard plain to see;
And to a weaver, given too
In writing, when the work to do
Is given out. The sheet must say
The details both of work and pay.

And where such matters may be seen
Shown on a self-working machine
It must declare the speed and size
Of the machinery likewise,
That every worker may be shown
What cash, each week, will be his own.

Children.

But as for working children, they
Must only work for half a day;
Early the half may be, or late,
Or else the times may alternate.

Jewesses.

For Jewish girls a special way
Makes Sunday stand for Saturday.

Overtime.

Of overtime, remember, none
May by young people, now, be done.
Two hours, and never more than two
Women, three times a week, may do,
But this, you will be glad to hear,
Not more than thirty days a year.
This is the rule for trades, except
Those where the things may spoil, if kept.
There sixty times a year you may
Be overworked two hours a day.

Notice of
Overtime.

Employers, when they mean to work
For extra hours, must never shirk
Notice to the Inspector, who
Will count how many times they do.

Outwork.

No child who has on any day
Done inside work must take away
Work to be done at home: and no
Young folk or women may do so
When they have worked a morning spell
And after dinner-time as well.

Laundries.

In laundries, little children may
Be kept at work ten hours a day.
But if you count the whole week through,
Not more than thirty hours may do.
Twelve hours in every twenty-four
Girls may be kept, and women more:
For fourteen hours the laundry hand
By law may at her wash-tub stand
With–that she may be kept alive–
A half-hour's break at every five.
If all the week of work you count,
The woman's hours to sixty mount.
Of overtime a couple, too,
She thirty days a year may do,
But not–the law's so much her friend–
For more than fourteen hours on end.

Ventilation
Gas-irons.

In laundries, too, I beg to state
There must be means to ventilate;
Nor may there be in any rooms
Gas-irons that give unwholesome fumes.

Fatal
Accidents.

When anyone by accident
Is killed, a notice must be sent
To a certifying surgeon, who
Has certain duties then to do.

Other
Accidents.

When boilers burst, or knife-blades slip,
When rollers crush a finger tip,
When bottles or when shuttles fly
And hurt the persons standing by,
In short, when any accident
Does so much harm as to prevent
The person hurt from being fit,
On one of three days after it,
To work five hours, there must be word
Sent the inspector what occurred.

Abstracts.

Factories, workshops, laundries, all
Must have a notice on the wall;
How many people in the place
Are working, and the cubic space;
Where surgeon and inspector live;
Worktimes and mealtimes it must give.

Obstructing
Inspectors.

Persons who hinder or delay
Inspectors, may be made to pay
Five pounds if done in full daylight
Or twenty pounds if done by night.

What to do
when the
law is
broken.

If any person gets to know
The laws are broken he should go
And write the details one and all
To the inspectors at Whitehall;
(Female inspectors letters meet
At 66, Victoria Street)
He need not sign if he prefers
To keep his name concealed—or hers.

Moral.

Such are the rules, which every day
Are broken, one or other way,
A thing the workers, if they knew
Could quickly put an ending to;
But some don't know and some don't care,
And some are always in a scare.

So overwork and underpay
Go gaily on from day to day,
And will, till those who work unite
To see their own affairs kept right.

CLEMENTINA BLACK.

Clementina Black on sweated industry

Clementina Black had early come to believe in the importance of a minimum wage and thus joined with others to campaign for this measure. In addition to her attempts to convince the Council to support publicly such legislation, Black endorsed the programme of the Anti-Sweating League, formed in 1906, to create a wage board system. The following selection is from a larger work, *Sweated Industry and the Minimum Wage*, published in 1907, with an introduction by A. G. Gardiner, who was chairman of the Executive Committee of the National Anti-Sweating League.*

This excerpt is interesting in that it is based upon her experiences as a social investigator, particularly among working women and girls. It indicates both her respect for this class and her realization that she could not completely bridge the gap which existed between her and the workers she wanted to help. It also illustrates her collectivist philosophy which was part of her feminist vision. Educated in Fabian Socialism, she emphasizes the role of the state as the protector of its workers. Although Black spent most of her adult life in seeking to improve the economic position of women, her feminist consciousness was broad enough to envision protection for all labourers – male and female and young and old.

❋

Chapter VI

SUMMARY

Home work–Factory work–The working girl–Her manners, virtues and code of honour–The woman into whom she developes–Shop assistants– . . . –Children–"Sweated" workers often producing high priced goods–Not drunken–Not idle–Not unskilful–Men as helpless, economically, as women–Sweating an invariable accompaniment of unregulated labour.

---

* From Clementina Black, *Sweated Industry and the Minimum Wage* (London, Duckworth & Co., 1907).

The preceding chapters do not profess to give anything like a general survey of the whole field of British labour. It has seemed wise for many reasons to confine myself to aspects with which I am, in a greater or less degree, personally familiar; and therefore the work of women, and of London women especially, looms rather large. But I hope that I have shown, by a sufficient range of instances, certain general truths. In trade after trade, men, women and children are exhibited working in the conditions which are indicated, comprehensively but vaguely, by the term "sweating." We have seen the dwelling of the homeworker robbed of every feature that makes a home, its narrow space littered with match boxes, or with shirts or trousers or paper bags—in any case transformed into one of the most comfortless of workshops. In some homes the rattle of the sewing machine forms a ceaseless accompaniment to the whole course of family life; in others, meals, such as they are, are eaten in the immediate neighbourhood of the glue pot or the paste pot; the smell of new cloth, the dust and fluff of flannelette pervade the room of the "finisher"; damp paper bags or damp cardboard boxes lie piled on beds; home, parents and children are all subservient to unintermittent and most unremunerative labour.

One step, but only one step, higher comes the factory "hand." We have seen girls filling pots with boiling jam, carrying to and fro heavy trays and stacking these trays in piles, two together raising, sometimes to above the height of their own heads, trays some of which weigh well over half a hundredweight. We have seen them, even when their work was not in itself heavy, worn out by the rapidity with which they repeat endlessly, day after day, and week after week, operations of mechanical monotony. Some glimpse has been given of those horrible intervals in which the semi-starvation of "full work" gives place to the acute privation of "slack time." The dangers, discomforts, hardships and exactions that must be borne if an employer chooses to inflict them, have been indicated, though but very inadequately; and the example of laundries and jam factories has served to suggest how far worse yet would be the conditions of factory operatives if the law did not intervene for their protection.

One thing I have not succeeded in picturing—and it is the thing which seems to me perhaps the most terrible of all: the change of the working girl into the working woman. I have not drawn the factory girl as I have known her and delighted in her, gay to "cheekiness," staunchly loyal, wonderfully uncomplaining, wonderfully ready to make allowances for "the governor" as long as he speaks her fair and shows consideration in trifles, but equally resolute to "pay him out," when once she is convinced of his meanness or spitefulness. Her language is devoid, to a degree remarkable even in our undemonstrative race, of any tenderness or emotion. She accepts an invitation with the ungracious formula: "I don't mind if I do." Upon the "mate" of her own sex, to whom she is so much more warmly devoted than to her "chap," she never bestows a word of endearment. "Hi, 'Liza, d'y' think I'm going to wait all night for you?" is the tone of her address to the friend with whom she will share her last penny or for whom she will pawn her last item of pawnable property. She speaks roughly to her relatives and aggressively to the world at large; she is no respecter of persons, and here eye for affection or insincerity is unerring. Condescend to her and she will "chaff" you off the field. But meet her on equal terms, help her without attempting to "boss" her, and within a month or two you will have won her unalterable allegiance; her face will light up at your coming; she will bear the plainest speech from you, and on occasion of emergency will obey implicitly your every command. Nor is she lacking in the fundamental parts of politeness. Here is an instance. Years ago, in the days when some of us still believed in the possibility of organising unskilled women, a member of the Dockers' Union sent me word that I should find it possible to walk at dinner time straight into the dining room of a certain factory and talk to the workers undisturbed, since at that hour both the foreman and the porter went home to their own meals. I went, accordingly, though I confess that I felt myself very much of a trespasser. As I mounted the extremely grimy stair to the dining room, I heard the loud voices of the girls. Their language was singularly vile. It did not, no doubt, mean very much to them; they used horrible words as the young of another class use slang. I went in and said my little say. After the first few words, most of them listened; several asked questions; a certain amount of conversation continued to go on. But while I was in the room—and, remember, I was a complete stranger to all of them—not one word was spoken which I could justly have felt to be offensive. I distributed my handbills, told them I hoped they would come to the meeting, and departed. As I went downstairs, I heard them relapsing into their hideous vernacular. But I could not help reflecting that they had shown the essence of good manners; and also that, if the literature of the eighteenth century is to be trusted, the same form of good

manners was far from being universal among those swearing country gentlemen who were the great grandfathers of our smooth spoken generation.[1]

The factory girl's code of honour is curiously like that of the school boy. In
no circumstances will she denounce a companion. To the governor or to the
forewoman she will lie freely if occasion demands. To those whom she
recognises as allies, she is truth itself. I do not recall one single instance, in
disputes between workers and employers, in which the tale told by working
girls has not been proved true in every detail. With employers, I am sorry to
say, this has often been by no means the case. Two qualities, in particular,
mark the factory girl of from sixteen to twenty: her exuberant spirits and
energy, and the invariable improvement in manner and language that follows
upon any sort of amelioration in her position. To watch the rapid development of refinement and gentleness consequent upon joining a good club is to
feel how sound is the national character and how lamentable the yearly waste
of admirable human material.

A few years pass, a very few, and these bright girls become apathetic,
listless women of whom at 35 it is impossible to guess whether their age is 40
or 50. They are tired out; they toil on, but they have ceased to look forward or
to entertain any hopes. The contrast between the factory girl and her mother
is perhaps the very saddest spectacle that the labour world presents. To be
the wife of a casual labourer, the mother of many children, living always in
too small a space and always in a noise, is an existence that makes of too many
women, in what ought to be the prime of their lives, mere machines of toil,
going on from day to day, with as little hope and as little happiness as the
sewing machine that furnishes one item in their permanent weariness.

We ascend another step and come to the shop assistants, the clerks and
the waitresses in restaurants. We find that these dapper young men and trim
young women whose hands and faces are so much cleaner and whose speech
and manners are so much smoother than those of the factory worker, are
scarcely better off in the matter of pay, and often absolutely worse off
in the matter of working conditions. The factory worker is at least free
after the factory closes, and, except in laundries, the law generally

---

[1] *It must not be assumed from the above anecdote that all factory girls are foul-mouthed. This was by no means true
even in the year after the Dock strike, and is much less true now. But I have no doubt there are still factories in which
the habit of foul speech is a sort of fashion.*

succeeds in bringing down the hours of work to something near a reasonable limit.

But the shop assistant is subject to rule during practically the whole of his or her working life; food, companions, dress, sleeping arrangements, hours of going to bed and of getting up, nay, the very medical man to be consulted in case of illness are thrust upon him without any choice of his own. The privilege, so dear to the natural man, of wearing an old coat and old slippers in the hours of relaxation, is not for the shop assistant; nor the modern diversion of experimenting with new and strange foods, nor the right of voting at elections, either municipal or parliamentary. The position combines, in short, the disagreeables of boarding school with those of domestic service, while failing to offer the pleasant features of either. It is indeed a moot point in my own mind whether it is not worse to be a shop assistant than a home-worker, supposing the home-worker to be a single woman. Personally, I would rather make cardboard boxes in silence and solitude, and buy for myself my own inferior bread and cheap tea. . . .

Last of all, we come to the children. In these days we are continually talking in tones of alarm about a declining birth rate and are at last seriously considering how to check the appalling infant mortality that makes an annual massacre of the innocents; but most of us are still very little awake to the sacrifice of childhood that is daily being made in our midst. We pass a pale child in the street, carrying a long bundle in a black wrapper, and the sight makes no impression. But, to those of us who have seen the under side of London, that little figure is a type of unremunerative toil, of stunted growth, of weakened vitality and of wasted school teaching: an example of that most cruel form of improvidence described by the French proverb as "eating our wheat as grass." Labour in childhood inevitably means, in nine cases out of ten, decadence in early manhood or womanhood; and the prevalence of it among ourselves is perhaps the most serious of national dangers. There is probably no branch of home work in which child labour is not involved, and but very few branches of retail trade. Our milk, our newspapers, our greengrocery are brought to us by small boys; young boys are out at all hours and in all weathers with parcel-delivering vans, and many and many a perambulator is pushed by a small girl whose chin is on a level with the handle. If, in 1901, there were, as the Interdepartmental Committee declare, *at least* 200,000 school children working for wages, and if, as seems practically certain, the number is larger now, can we wonder that so many grown up workers have remained inefficient, incompetent and listless? We cannot have grain, if we choose to eat the wheat in the blade.

We see, then, that large bodies of British workpeople are, in these early years of the twentieth century, extremely overworked and underpaid. These evils are not, as is so often declared, a result of cheap selling. One of the worst examples of underpayment in the Sweated Industries Exhibition was a lady's combination garment, of nainsook, the selling price of which was 22s.; and much of the work produced by the underpaid is sold at a good price to the well-to-do. On the other hand, under a well organised factory system, goods that are sold at a very low price are sometimes produced by workers receiving comparatively high wages. Nor is it true that any large proportion of these ill paid workers are either drunken or idle, or yet incompetent. Incompetent, indeed, they eventually become, if they are starved, physically and mentally, for a long enough period; but many of them remain competent for a surprising number of years. Very many of them are pathetically industrious, and by no means all are unskilled. Neither my reader nor I, for instance, could cover a racquet ball so that it would pass muster when inspected by the paymaster; it is improbable that either of us could cover an umbrella, and pretty certain that neither could make a passable artificial rose of even the poorest description. The driver of a motor omnibus is—in theory at least, and often in practice—a highly skilled mechanic; but his skill does not enable him (his trade union being still comparatively young and weak) to retain his freedom of action nor to resist the most exhausting and harassing conditions of labour.

The evil is thus not confined to women, nor to home-workers, nor to any class or trade. Nor is it confined to any one country. Nearly every instance quoted could be matched from Germany and from America. "Sweating," in short, invariably tends to appear wherever and whenever industry is not either highly organised or else stringently regulated by law.

Suggestions for further reading

In addition to the works on social and political feminism cited in the footnotes, Constance Rover's *Love, Morals and the Feminists* (1970) raises some interesting questions about feminist acceptance of both societal proscriptions for women and traditional moral codes. An article by Harriet Warm Schupf, 'Single Women and Social Reform in Mid-Nineteenth Century England: The Case of Mary Carpenter' (*Victorian Studies* (March 1974)), discusses social feminism in the mid-nineteenth century. For the suffrage movement, see also Andrew Rosen's *Rise up, Women! The Militant Campaign of the Women's Social and Political Union. 1903–1914* (1974), and the study on 'radical suffragists' by Jill Liddington and Jill Norris, *One Hand Tied Behind Us. The Rise of the Women's Suffrage Movement* (1978). For a general comparative study of feminism, see Richard J. Evans, *The Feminists. Women's Emancipation Movements in Europe, America and Australasia. 1840–1920* (1977). For a study on the opposition to women's higher education in the Victorian era, see Joan N. Burstyn's *Victorian Education and the Ideal of Womanhood* (1980). For general works on women in society, see Sheila Rowbotham's *Hidden from History* (1974) and Patricia Branca's *Women in Europe Since 1750* (1978). For two useful anthologies, see Patricia Hollis, *Women in Public: The Women's Movement 1850–1900. Documents of the Victorian Women's Movement* (1979), and Janet Murray, *Strong-Minded Women and Other Lost Voices from Nineteenth-Century England* (1982). To supplement Drake's work on trade unionism, see Sheila Lewenhak, *Women and Trade Unions* (1977). *Married Women's Work* (orig. 1915), edited by Clementina Black, has recently been reprinted, with a new introduction by Ellen F. Mappen (1983).

Further Pamphlets published by the
Women's Research and Resources Centre

Some Processes in Sexist Education
by Ann Marie Wolpe £1.00

**Inspiration and Drudgery: Notes on
Literature and Domestic Labour in the
19th Century**
by Sarah Elbert and Marion Glastonbury £0.70

**Girls Will Be Girls: Sexism and Juvenile Justice
in a London Borough**
by Maggie Casburn £0.60

**'Black Friday': Violence Against Women in the
Suffragette Movement**
by Caroline Morrell £1.95

Obtainable from your local bookshop or direct by post from
1a Gladys Road, London NW6 2PU